How Great Leaders UNCOVER PROBLEMS and Unleash Performance

BLIND SPOTS

MARISA MURRAY

USA TODAY Bestselling Author

Author: Marisa Murray
Editor: Jonathan Jordan
Cover design: Susan Schultz
Graphic Designer: Maksym Sopov

ISBN: 978-1-7380301-2-5   Hardcover
      978-1-7380301-1-8   eBook
      978-1-7380301-0-1   Paperback

ABOUT THE AUTHOR

Marisa Murray is the Amazon #1 bestselling author of Work Smart and Iterate. She is also coauthor of the *USA Today* bestseller *The Younger Self Letters*. Marisa is a sought-after TEDx speaker who has made it her mission to help people uncover their blind spots and achieve their full potential. With a  passion for leadership development and a talent for storytelling, Marisa has written extensively on the topic of blind spots and the role they play in our lives.

Marisa is the CEO and founder of Leaderley International and a former Partner with Accenture and Vice President at Bell Canada who works with Fortune 500 organizations to help them identify and overcome the obstacles that have been holding them back.

Leaderley International is an award-winning organization recognized as one of the Top 10 Emerging Executive Coaching Companies for 2023 by *Manage HR* magazine[1] and as a top

---

[1] www.managehrmagazine.com/leaderley-international

entrepreneur, influential leader, and innovator on *Brainz Magazine*'s CREA Global Award list for 2023[2].

Whether through her books, her coaching engagements, 360s, or speaking engagements, Marisa has a gift for connecting with people and inspiring them to make positive changes in their lives.

Marisa is a Professional Certified Coach (PCC), holds an MBA from Queen's University, and is a professional engineer from the University of Waterloo. When not working, she can be found spending time with her husband and two sons. She loves travelling, reading, skiing, and sharing her love of yoga with her family and friends.

 Connect with Marisa on LinkedIn
LinkedIn.com/in/murraymarisa
or at www.leaderley.com.

---

[2] www.brainzmagazine.com/crea-2023/marisa-murray

DEDICATION

To my clients, who entrust me with the honour of accompanying them on their professional journeys. Together, we explore how to become better leaders by discovering our blind spots to uncover our truth. Through your stories, I see myself.

To my incredible sons, Tobias and Theodore, whose insightful questions over the last two decades have helped me uncover my beliefs, biases, and blind spots at home. You raised me while I thought I was raising you.

And to Paul, my wonderful husband, who provides endless encouragement and support. You are my rock. None of my books would exist without you.

TABLE OF
CONTENTS

SPECIAL BONUS FOR YOU

If you're an executive, you understand the importance of valuable feedback That's why FeedbackFriend, was built.

A game-changing AI tool revolutionizing how you gather feedback to unlock your next level of performance.

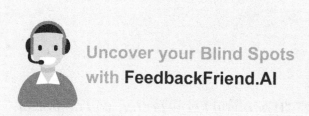

Uncover your Blind Spots
with **FeedbackFriend.AI**

Your **AI-powered** Personal Feedback Assistant!
To accelerate your development, look no further!

Go to **FEEDBACKFRIEND.AI**
to revolutionize your development.
Your blind spot is your breakthrough!

FeedbackFriend allows you to collect anonymous feedback from 5 to 15 people **For FREE** to uncover your top strengths and development areas to <u>enable you</u> to reflect on your potential blind spots!

Try it now for free here: www.feedbackfriend.ai

"When you know better, you do better."

—Maya Angelou

INTRODUCTION

The Iceberg in the Fog

From the classroom to the silver screen, the tragic tale of the "unsinkable" ship known as the RMS *Titanic* serves as an ominous warning.

But what really led to the sinking of the *Titanic*?

Everyone knows it hit an iceberg, but for over a century, there have been a myriad of theories behind *why* the ship struck the iceberg. These range from accusations of the captain being drunk to a missing pair of binoculars.

Add to this the paradoxical eyewitness accounts from survivors and other crew members who recalled it was a very clear night. From the lookout, there should have been at least fifty miles of visibility, even without binoculars. Yet the lookout officers testified to the presence of a haze on the night of April 14, 1912, which kept them from seeing the iceberg until they were almost right on top of it. Both accounts cannot be true.

Or can they?

A six-year investigation by British historian Tim Maltin seems to have uncovered the reason behind this paradox and why the lookouts didn't see the iceberg in time:

In an interview with *Science Digest*, Mr. Maltin described a miraging haze, which impacts the amount of air you can see through on a clear night.

This haze is caused by a phenomenon called "thermal inversion," created when warmer air sits on top of cold air, causing an optical effect where the lookout officers could have been able to see as far as eighty miles ahead. At the same time, the haze sitting along the water may have had the same colouring as the iceberg itself, hiding it in plain sight.[3]

In the corporate boardroom, the infamous sinking of the *Titanic* has become a metaphorical warning to leaders of the importance of looking ahead and not making assumptions and an example of how details can sink the best-laid plans—literally. Like the

---

[3] Antony Ashkenaz, "Titanic Mystery Solved: Expert Finds What 'Really' Caused Sinking after Six-Year Probe," Daily Express, June 22, 2022, https://www.express.co.uk/news/science/1628821/titanic-mystery-solved-experts-finds-real-cause-sinking-optical-phenomenon-iceberg.

iceberg hiding in the haze, the most dangerous problems any organization faces are the ones they don't see.

The most dangerous problems organization's face are the ones they don't see.

Yet perhaps the lesson is even more profound. What if everyone involved in the maiden trip of the *Titanic* was looking ahead? What more could they have done? How could the story have changed?

Before becoming a corporate executive coach, I was an engineer, relying on my analytical skills to prepare, plan, and predict issues so the services and solutions our teams created were robust and reliable. From an engineering design standpoint, I find the story of the *Titanic* fascinating because of the intention of the engineers to build an "unsinkable" ship. This intention permeated every aspect of the design, including the ship's sixteen watertight compartments, which could be sealed remotely—an incredible innovation for the time.

This level of precaution was likely considered overkill. By design, the ship would have been able to remain afloat if four of the watertight containers were damaged. Unfortunately, the fatal impact on the starboard side compromised *six* compartments.

To some, executive coaching may seem like a long way away from engineering design, but I draw from my engineering background more often than you might think. It helps me support my clients by helping them look at their leadership from a design angle, asking, "What's working? What's not working? How can this be made better?" Every day, corporate executives make design decisions about how they will show up as leaders and what values they want to exhibit. These are important engineering questions, just like the engineers of the *Titanic* likely asked themselves many questions as they sought to fulfill their intention of crafting the strongest ship possible.

The difficulty with intention is that it's only *part* of the story.

Hopefully, what brings you to this book is your desire to ask even better questions, to achieve better impact. I suspect you know the answers to the simple questions. Every client I serve in my coaching practice is senior enough to know the "right way" to behave in the work environment. Yet once they find themselves in icy waters, the context can create confusion and fog, resulting in **blind spots**.

So how do you fix the problem you can't see? How do you pivot your organization to avoid its icebergs? Unlike the plans you have for responding to industry trends, winning client contracts, or managing risks in the market, your blind spots are the icebergs hiding in the haze, able to damage your ship at its core.

You can't prevent blind spots from happening any more than the crew of the *Titanic* could prevent icebergs. But what if you knew how to uncover the blind spots hiding in your team? And even better, how to address them? How could it change your trajectory toward where you want to go?

Finding and Defining Blind Spots

My first book, *Work Smart*, focused on the formulas and strategies that have helped me and others be more successful. *Iterate!*—my second book—was written and released during the COVID-19 pandemic and centered on encouraging leaders to pivot in the midst of turbulent times and be more *iteractive*.

When I first sat down to write this book, my plan was to talk about achieving leadership success without stress. But the more I thought about my interactions with my coaching clients, the more I realized it is my clients' blind spots that cause them the most stress. My clients are very senior leaders, skilled and experienced in their roles. When they see a problem, they excel at addressing it.

But with blind spots, they can sense there is a problem—but they can't see it. They recognize that something isn't working and that they are not having the impact they would like, but they don't know exactly *what* it is or how to address it.

This is how it feels to have blind spots. Whether they belong to you or someone on your team, the damage they inflict is easier to *feel* than it is to *see*. The root cause can be catastrophic if it is left unaddressed—or noticed too late.

By definition, blind spots are difficult to spot. They often hide in plain sight because they are closely linked to our strengths. They are often behaviours masquerading as strengths while causing unintended consequences in our collaborations. In time, they then erode our performance. The way I define them in my work is "the gap between one's intention and one's impact."

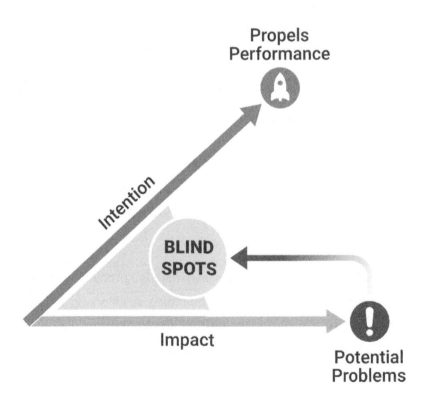

The key to identifying a specific blind spot is this impact piece because you can't know your impact without asking other people. We all tend to be hyperfocused on our own intentions. We make decisions and act upon our intentions because they are clear to us. We forget our intentions are invisible to others—they can only experience our *impact* on them. If our impact is different from our intention, we know that we have a blind spot.

It is kind of like how astronomers find black holes. They locate them by detecting the radiation emitted when swirling matter falls into them. Blind spots can be located when the leader's impact is off course, on a different trajectory than the intention they are striving for. Depending on the severity of the blind spot, the gap between intention and impact can become a massive performance eroder for the organization. Not to mention, the severity is amplified by our relative level of responsibility within the organization.

The best leaders are always trying to narrow the gap between their intention and impact, so the two end up being correlated. Doing so requires proactively seeking out your specific blind spots. To do this, you have to develop a clear, unfiltered understanding of your impact. You gain this not from your own perspective, since that's usually where the blind spot lives, but through the eye of the beholder—that is, the people being impacted.

I have completed thousands of interviews for hundreds of client programs since founding my company, Leaderley, to help my clients identify their blind spots. One of the biggest pieces of this process is collecting impact statements from their key stakeholders. These impact statements are unlike any feedback they have ever received. Impact statements are more transparent and detailed, often revealing misunderstandings and perceptions my clients were not aware of.

When I review the data with my clients, it is not unusual for them to feel confused, hurt, offended, betrayed, or disoriented at first as they become aware of other people's interpretations of their behaviours, because it can be so different from their intention. I often need to reassure them that this exercise is only for our coaching bubble, so they need not worry about implications. I encourage them to let the feedback wash over them as we look for insights that will help them see situations entirely from others' perspectives.

This includes helping them receive the impact statements as "true for the stakeholder" even when they disagree with the perspectives or when the details embedded in the statements are skewed. With support and a heavy dose of empathy, my clients come to see they can take accountability for the impact they are having. With this accountability, they can make efforts to change their impact, keeping in mind that blind spots are not their fault, and any negative implications were not intentional.

"The truth will set you free,
but first it will piss you off."
—Gloria Steinem

Whether they take them too personally or are apathetic toward the impact statements, the focus is to help clients recognize the importance of the data. I try to encourage them to perceive the data points as neutral as possible, with no emotional charge. It's not negative or positive—it's just data. Data to help them grow. Data to expose their blind spots. Data that enables them to close the gap between their intentions and their impact.

You can think of the impact statements like a magnifying glass that allows you to zoom in on the details you've overlooked in yourself. The difficult part is that this can be painful. It forces you to look closely at actions you've justified or overlooked. You may discover there are problems with your leadership that you didn't even realize were there.

The good news? Every client who has gone through this process has later told me how the impact statements were critical to their transformation. The ability to understand their true impact on others enabled them to *choose* new behaviours and actions more strategically. They also ended up learning as much (or more) about their stakeholders as they did about themselves, which ultimately deepened these important relationships.

Intention and Impact

One of the most infamous blind spots of the *Titanic* was the failure to have enough lifeboats for all passengers. The intention of the ship's designers was to design a ship so safe, so impervious to sinking, that the presence of any lifeboats would be redundant. The intention was never to put people in danger—but they made a fatally false assumption.

As you will see in the first blind spot we cover, false assumptions driven by good intentions can create unintentional impacts.

The impact of *Titanic*'s loss was devastating. The most tragic being the loss of human life—1,500 people out of the 2,240 passengers on board died. There was also a terrible loss from the business perspective. The ship cost $7.5 million to build in 1912— that's nearly $225 million today. Neither the financial cost nor reputational damage to the British shipping company, White Star Line, were ever recouped.

All the clients I work with have good intentions. They are not satisfied with being just good leaders—they want to be *great* leaders. You know those people who are amazing at their jobs but are always looking to get even better? That's who I work with. More often than not, what is preventing them from being even better are the blind spots driving a wedge between their intention and their impact.

There are also circumstances that create blind spots for a leader. One of the most frequent scenarios is when C-suite leaders are recruited into an executive role in a new company or division. It is so common that I have a specific coaching program designed for these leaders called "integration coaching." This is most applicable when a senior leader is in the midst of climbing up the steep learning curve involved in a new role. They're immersed in—and sometimes overwhelmed with—the new environment's culture, its people, and its ways of working. To set this executive up for success, many of my clients will engage me in an executive coaching mandate to assist with the executive's integration.

Why? Because a new corporation, division, or role can be a minefield of blind spots for a new leader.

To be transparent, this is the type of coaching I wish I'd had in my last corporate position. When I left Accenture after fifteen years, I joined a new executive team, and—to make a long story short—I did a lot wrong and ended up quitting within a year.

In hindsight, I can trace everything back to my own professional blind spots.

For starters, I came into the new company with an attitude of "You hired me because of my expertise, so you want me to change things!" The problem was I didn't yet have a clear understanding of the new company's capabilities or culture. In fact, I falsely assumed I was hired to replicate the culture of my previous company.

I didn't understand the people, how they were prepared, or how the history of the company shaped their thinking. When I couldn't influence others the way I expected to, all I could see was what was "wrong" with everybody else. I focused on what I perceived as flaws in the company rather than taking the time to understand its strengths.

For example, I felt immense frustration because I believed my team was not as client-centric as they needed to be. This was partially true, but what I could not see was their incredible commitment to internal operational excellence. My core beliefs were driving me to conclude everything about them was wrong because it was different from what I was used to.

What I couldn't see then—that I can see now—is how I could have worked within the qualities of the organizational culture. I could have found a way to apply my team's operations-centric strengths toward client-centric impact. Blinded by my own beliefs, I instead concluded I could not be successful and decided to quit.

After quitting, I remember sitting on my bedroom floor feeling confused, asking myself, "What the heck happened?" and trying to figure out what I would do next. Should I go out to get another executive position? After that experience, I was worried that I would simply repeat the same mistake.

I felt like a failure, even though I knew I had a track record of being a great leader. This ultimately began my quest to unpack this ambiguous mission called "leadership" and make it my mission to help my clients become "Leaderley." I believe that being *Leaderley* is the highest compliment, since the journey to your best leader is also the journey to your best life.

It's only in retrospect, from all the client work, that I've been able to recognize my blind spots from my previous positions. In the stories of others, I heard the echoes of my own mistakes. Now I can see how my blind spots skewed my impact and led me to run into my own personal iceberg.

This is what I want to help you avoid through this book. If you are feeling plagued by your culture, collaborators, or environment, it's really easy to blame others like I did. But playing the blame game only reinforces our own misaligned beliefs or false assumptions. We end up justifying our actions instead of looking at how they may have contributed to the problem.

With the benefit of both hindsight and foresight (by inviting insights from others), I've learned to hold up the mirror and see my own blind spots. And I'm dedicated to helping others find theirs so that they close the gap between intention and impact. Doing so allows all of us to move our trajectory toward our greatest success and carve a path to our desired future.

Addressing Your Blind Spots

By now you may have in mind a number of other people you believe may benefit from identifying their blind spots. Perhaps these people are on your team, and you have been trying to mentor and coach them. Before we move on, I want to share one more story from my personal life that I believe will be significant for you in this journey.

When I gave birth to my eldest son, I was working as a management consultant. My lens at work was fixated on high performance and implementing best practices to achieve predictably positive outcomes. As such, I saw everything as a project—everything was a transformation.

So, there I was with this new baby in my arms, overcome with love. I knew I had never loved anything more in my life. My heart was bursting full of good will as I said to myself, "There's nothing I want to do better than parent this child. I'm going to be the best parent the world has ever seen, because this is the most important thing to me." Then I whispered into his tiny ear: "I'm going to make you perfect."

Maybe you can already see the problem. Maybe you've even lived through this exact scenario. The next few years—more like five years if I'm totally honest—I approached parenting with a management consultant mindset. I became an obsessed parenting monster, reading everything on child psychological development, waking him up to take him to the library at three months old, teaching him sign language before he could talk, playing classical music in the house 24/7, and doing all the "right" things to make him be what I had determined was a successful child.

My intentions were good, of course. I wanted to be a great parent, and I wanted my child to be successful and happy. What's wrong with that?

But the impact of my actions became skewed by my own false assumptions regarding success as a parent. Eventually, my son started self-expressing—and it turned out he had his *own* ideas and agendas. Who knew, right?

My eldest son has a strong character, and the more I held on to my own view of his success and interests, the more the gap between intention and impact widened. I remember one specific fight we had when he told me he wanted to be a professional goalie in the NHL. I told him it was a bad idea, not because he was bad at hockey but because *I* knew nothing about hockey. Instead, I thought he should go into engineering, get his MBA, and go into business—because *I* knew how to do that. He looked at me and said, "Isn't it supposed to be my choice?"

Over the coming years, both my kids pointed out how I couldn't know what they wanted because I'm not them. I was blinded by what *I* wanted them to want—which is the opposite of being a good parent. I learned being a successful parent was about providing them with the resources they needed to follow their own development journey, not copy mine. It was not my job to predetermine their path but to be their enabler—to treat them with the respect they deserved as whole, complete, and separate human beings. This made me a different mother, shifting me from *controlling* them to *collaborating* with them.

Leadership is like that too. Leadership is all about your ability to collaborate and join forces with others to achieve an outcome. There's a temptation to want to *fix* people and presume you know what the fix is. I'm sure you have some great hypotheses about what your team member or culture needs, but you alone cannot change people into what you want them to be.

The work begins with you—just like I learned with parenting. The first step in transforming your organization and leading your team to more success is to help everyone illuminate **their own** blind spots. Collect and reflect on the necessary data to see how *you* need to evolve so you can then enable *them* to evolve. It may result in redefining your views of success, updating your core beliefs, and confronting your false assumptions.

The work you do in spotting your blind spots will make you far more effective in helping your team address theirs. If you can do that, your impact will correlate with your intention.

Blind Spots

We All Have One...or Seven

As you've probably figured out by now, it wasn't just one blind spot that caused the *Titanic* disaster—there were many at play. Some were completely out of anyone's control, like the iceberg-concealing haze caused by the weather. Others were completely in their control, such as the decision to not have enough lifeboats for every passenger. It's also likely that a better understanding of surface fog may have changed the outcome.

We all have blind spots. I'm willing to bet this isn't news to you. Great leaders not only recognize they have blind spots, but they have a desire to find and address them, in addition to providing their team members with the resources to do the same.

As an executive coach, helping others find and fix their blind spots has been the heartbeat of my work for the better part of a decade now. It's difficult but fun work because I get to walk together with my clients in closing the gap between their intention and their impact.

In this book, I want to help you identify some of the areas where you probably don't know what you don't know. For this discovery, it's helpful to have an external perspective and a framework for reference. Over the course of serving hundreds of coaching clients, I've seen seven blind-spot areas that pop up time and time again:

1 False Assumptions

2 Unhealthy Detachment

3 Differing Views of Success

4 Outdated Core Beliefs

5 Unconscious Habits

6 Triggers from Past Pain

7 Mismatched Mindsets

That's not to say these are the only blind spots, but they are the most common ones I see inflicting the greatest damage on people, teams, and organizations. As you'll soon see, many of these blind-spot areas have overlaps with one another—false assumptions can create differing views of success, outdated core beliefs can lead to unconscious habits, and so on.

As Farnam Street founder Shane Parrish and Farnam Street managing editor Rhiannon Beaubien observe in their book *The Great Mental Models*, "In life and business, the person with the fewest blind spots wins. Removing blind spots means we see, interact with, and move closer to understanding reality. We think better. And thinking better is about finding simple processes that help us work through problems from multiple dimensions and perspectives, allowing us to better choose solutions that fit what matters to us."[4]

Learning from Other Leaders

I can still hear the words of my amazing TED Talk coach, Sam Horn, when she reviewed the first draft of my talk: "Your talk has

---

[4] Rhiannon Beaubien and Shane Parrish, *The Great Mental Models Volume 1: General Thinking Concepts*, (Ottawa, Canada: Latticework Publishing, 2019), 19.

too much *teaching* in it and not enough *learning*. Stop trying to teach; tell stories instead. No one wants to be taught, but people really want to learn. We humans learn best through stories."

For blind spots in particular, the best way I know to shed light on them is to share some stories so we can learn from each other. When facing blind spots, there can be a temptation to believe the current situation you're facing is unique. Challenging, yes—but not unique. This is really great news because it means others have faced the same challenges posed by these blind spots and come out the other side more successful by bringing their intentions into alignment with their impact. In fact, I think you will be both encouraged and challenged to see just how common these blind spots are.

Throughout the rest of this book, we'll walk through each of these blind-spot areas one by one and examine how they displayed themselves through real-life case studies. We'll let these stories do the teaching. Since each of these blind spots can have nuances to them, each chapter will feature three distinct case studies to show those nuances. As you would expect, names and some details have been changed to protect the privacy of individuals and their organizations, but otherwise, the stories represent true lived experiences by people just like you.

More than anything else, these case studies should provide you with some tangible examples of how these blind spots manifest themselves. Some of them may hit closer to home for you than others. Reading over the list above, perhaps you already recognize some of these in your team, but you're not sure how to address them. That's alright—the case studies will also provide you with some examples of how others have gone through the coaching process to define their blind spots and address them.

Perhaps you're picking up this book because the environment around you is already filled with crushing tension, resistance, and friction. Maybe there's so much "haze" that you can't see the icebergs you're about to collide with. Maybe the collision has already happened, and you're worried you don't have enough lifeboats.

That's alright! The fact that you recognize this is the first step to clearing the fog. My hope is that these stories will allow you to connect the dots with your own situation and capture insights about the blind spots within your team and organization. When you can face those insights with a bit of deliberate courage, it will help you and your team evolve into the next greatest version of yourselves.

Navigating corporate politics, repairing relationships, or changing perceptions is not as difficult as you think. It's actually pretty intuitive once you've identified the blind spots causing you pain. It doesn't have to feel hard!

What *can* be hard is being open and courageous enough to face your blind spots. Like with my parenting journey, this isn't something you as a leader can manhandle and force through the pipeline like another project. It's not about processes or structures; it's about developing the trust, faith, and patience to face the unknown.

The best news is this: because there tends to be overlaps between these seven blind-spot areas, it means there is a compounding effect. As you address one, you often end up fixing others along the way. Furthermore, when someone is able to define their blind spots and work on them, they not only improve themselves—they end up improving their teams and their organizations as a whole.

The only requirements here are for you to be fearless enough to seek out and reflect on the data. If you can do this, you can objectively determine what changes need to be made to improve the outcomes—without being tainted by your own blind spots.

As we begin this journey together, let me give you some encouragement from my experiences. Many of my clients who have gone through this have ended up loving it. So much so they keep coming back to go through it all again every few years. I even had a couple of clients who wanted me to get impact statements from their spouses, kids, and siblings to identify their blind spots at home; others simply ask better questions and get the feedback themselves.

My hope for you is to come out the other side of this book saying, "I was blind but now I see," because you learn how to spot your own blind spots, and you proactively address them instead of being reactive to the consequences they create. Finding and facing them is the most difficult part of the journey—course-correcting is not the hard part.

Due to the haze effect, the lookout officers on the *Titanic* had less than one minute to communicate the presence of the iceberg, and it was simply too late for the ship to course-correct. With only a little more forewarning, the story of the *Titanic* could have been very different—the ship could have completed a triumphant maiden voyage.

Finding and facing your blind spots can change your story by transforming your impact. Blind spots have immense power when they stay hidden. It's only in exposing them that we get to take back control and determine our own destiny. The cost of ignoring blind spots is massive. The payoff for fixing them is priceless.

As I mentioned before, many of these blind-spot areas overlap and share common themes with one another. For this reason, we'll begin our journey looking at the one that may have the most overlaps with the others—false assumptions.

YOUR NOTES

....

....

....

....

....

....

....

....

....

....

....

....

....

....

....

....

"What are you ASSUMING to be true?"

FALSE ASSUMPTIONS

Simple definition:	Things people do or ways they behave when they act on missing or inaccurate information.
Root cause:	People's behaviour is influenced by notions that *appear* true to them because more accurate or complete information is missing from their decision-making process.
Often results in:	Misalignment, frustration, conflict

How do you figure out if someone is running on a false assumption? How do you get into someone else's head and help them discover their own assumptions? What if by figuring out their false assumptions—or even your own—you could discover and address other blind spots surrounding you?

It sounds like professional telepathy—and it is a bit. All blind spots are sneaky, especially false assumptions. They like to masquerade as truth, and they tend to morph into core beliefs. When it's our own false assumptions, it is easy for us to justify and ignore the damage they cause. Since all assumptions begin to feel like the "truth," we don't question them like we might other behaviours.

Like other blind spots, false assumptions are embedded in people's "operating system," and like a computer virus, they often go unnoticed until the damage is done. A whole book could probably be written just on this one blind spot because of how many shapes it can take. If you're going to start anywhere with identifying your blind spots, questioning your assumptions and the assumptions of your team is a great place to begin.

Staying with our computer analogy, you have to examine your mind's operating system, which drives your perspective, decision-making, and behaviours. An "upgrade" of this operating system—and every application running on it—is required to make it work better. As a leader, this is even more important because your thinking guides more than your individual behaviours; it guides an entire team.

To help us see some of the ways false assumptions can play out, we'll look at three specific case studies where someone's false assumptions were distorting their intentions and wreaking havoc on their impact. As you read these, ask yourself, "Which one of these do I relate to the most? Which one have I seen before, and how did I deal with it? How is this currently showing up for me, my team, and the organization?"

 # David: The Difference Maker

Meet David, the "Difference Maker." The first thing you need to know about David is he's a bit of a unicorn because he is both deeply technical yet charismatic with clients. He's the kind of person who always went to the best schools and was in the top of the class—the smartest guy in the room. Before joining the technology company (where he's now a partner and member of the core leadership team), he spent years at other tech companies and came up the ranks due to his intelligence and technical prowess.

This blend of skills has put him in a position where he's responsible for sales, even though when you talk to him, he doesn't strike you as a "sales" guy. When I first gathered impact statements about David, there was wide agreement and praise for how he establishes rapport with clients in particular. The CEO even remarked on his knack for accurately reading clients, predicting their needs, and bringing the right technical solutions to them.

He's the kind of guy who listens when you say, "I like a good bottle of rum," and then takes note of what *specific* brand of rum you like—the one that's *impossible* to get. Then the day you sign the contract—*voilá*—the bottle of rum appears at your door. His amazing ability to retain details, combined with his kindness, creates a brand of client intimacy that draws people to him. This is what makes him a true Difference Maker.

He's also a Difference Maker with team members. People have consistently agreed that he is an attentive listener, a great communicator, energetic, and makes people feel seen and heard. He's the type who will look at a problem that's got everyone on the project stuck, study it for thirty seconds, and come up with the solution to get the team back on track.

In short, any company would love to have him on its executive team. So maybe you're wondering what the problem was.

The technical explanation for the problem was that he was just getting really, really *pissed off.*

David was one of the firm's managing partners, and the others started to notice a shift in his behaviour. He became progressively more aggressive and dysfunctional in their weekly meetings. He would come in immediately disgruntled, frustrated, and argumentative.

Part of this was obvious—David was incredibly overworked. He had a ton of responsibilities, even when compared to the other partners. As a result, he was dropping balls—which was far out of the ordinary for him—and they pointed this out.

"Well, I'm dropping balls because look at all this stuff I'm doing!" he argued.

"Then you need to delegate more," they all advised him. "You need to develop your team. You need to scale yourself."

Yet he consistently discounted this advice because his perspective was that they didn't know what they were talking about. *I'm the only one who can do all these things*, he thought. *And frankly, they should thank their lucky stars I'm here to do them.*

You're probably starting to see the false assumption emerge here. While he wouldn't say it in these exact words, David had a series of false assumptions driving his behaviours:

"I'm different."

"I'm special."

"People need me everywhere."

"No one can do things like me."

The way he verbalized this to me was to say, "These partner meetings are driving me crazy because I feel unappreciated for everything I've done—and now I'm being blamed for the problems. It's all pissing me off, and I just want to quit."

Now, mind you, these revelations didn't come to light until all the impact statements had been collected and analyzed to find insights into what was creating the gap between his intention and his impact. Remember, the gap between intention and impact is where the blind spot hides, and this was definitely true for David.

Several statements, in particular, revealed the negative impact he was having despite his good intentions:

> *"David is so talented in terms of his instincts, creativity, and spontaneity that he tends to underestimate the time and energy that may be required to lead a more planned and coordinated effort with other groups."*

This revealed another one of David's false assumptions: "Everyone else should be able to problem solve as quickly as me. And if they can't, I just need to do it for them."

> *"David has very good instincts and intuition, which enables him to be attentive and sensitive. However, this can also make him overly emotional or reactive to situations, which tends to create intense emotions and drama for him...without fully considering its relative priority or criticality. This can consume other people's time on his issues based on his mood at the moment."*

False assumption: "Everyone else needs to care with the same intensity about the same things and at the same moment as I do."

"David is obviously busy, so it is not always easy to get his time, but more than his time, it can also be hard to capture his attention, maintain his interest, and remain a priority for him...This makes it difficult for his people to build what he wants since the team benefits from his presence on a more consistent basis."

False assumption: "So many people need me; there's not enough time to give to everyone equally. They'll come find me if it's really necessary.

What I found interesting about David's case was how there was some truth to his false assumptions. He *is* special. People *do* need him everywhere. There was a level of legitimacy to the assumptions because each one was directly connected to his strengths. No wonder they were so hard to see!

What makes them false assumptions isn't that the statements themselves are false—but the fact that they lead to a false *conclusion* and the wrong leadership behaviours.

He assumed his skills were so unique to himself that it would be impossible to coach others to develop the same skills. He also assumed that if he was already dropping balls in this state, delegating responsibilities would surely lead to even *more* balls being dropped—which he then believed he would be blamed for.

Furthermore, it was noted how this fear of blame led David to blame others. He was transferring the negative energy of his false assumptions onto others without realizing it.

At the start of everything, David's general thinking was "It's them, not me." Eventually, through processing the impact statements and questioning the validity of his assumptions, he was able to make the shift to "It's not them. It's me. I don't know what I want."

David made this shift by replacing his false assumptions with some fresh perspective. First, we started at a personal level—he needed to start having more fun at work. He needed to see how much enjoyment he could actually get from developing others instead of just solving all the problems himself and "saving" people.

Next, we looked at the team level—where the impact statements allowed him to see specific examples of when he had been dramatic and self-oriented. He was able to empathize and understand that not every situation was about him. He gained awareness by realizing how, as a leader, his behaviour amplified the behaviours of his team. In other words, if he's in a bad mood, then it doesn't just impact his own productivity but the productivity of a *hundred* other people.

Finally, we looked at an organizational level. For the longest time, he said his motivation in joining the partnership was so the company could be the best in their market, and he had attributed this to himself. "We're going to be the best because *I* am here."

Now, he's made the shift to take the weight of this assumption off his own shoulders and say, "We're going to be the best because of how we nurture, train, develop, and serve our clients as a *team*."

Today, David is still the Difference Maker, but in a different way. He's so much more attuned to the skillsets of others and applying his intellect and creativity to how *they* can contribute to solving problems and serving clients. As a passionate person, he used to direct his passion in a way where he would exaggerate and catastrophize the situation. Now he can direct his passion in a healthier direction to build up others, which is healthier for everyone.

All of this took place over the course of about eighteen months. No one likes to be confronted with their blind spots and facing them is hard work. Early in the process, David told me it was too stressful for him, and he needed to take a break from coaching. He came back a month later, then needed another break. Eventually, though, he asked to extend our coaching sessions so he could solidify his new mindset and recognize his false assumptions the next time they showed up.

He went from "wanting to quit" to "loving his work again," which was a pretty exciting shift he attributes to this process. As a result, David has become a huge advocate for coaching. To this day, he regularly sends me more people from his organization for me to help.

Isaac: The Intellect

A senior strategic advisor at a consulting firm, Isaac had over thirty-five years of experience in the industry when I started working with him. Needless to say, he brought a wealth of experience to his work: strategic thinking, financial acumen, and deep analytical skills he leveraged to develop powerful insights. Besides longevity in his career, he also displayed incredible intellectual horsepower, which is why I call him "The Intellect." He himself admits he can be a bit of a workaholic because he finds his work so intellectually stimulating.

His role is unique in the consulting world because, while he is on the executive team for his company, he often serves as an interim chief strategy officer for other companies during various transformations, such as mergers and acquisitions.

Isaac first approached me for coaching because he was getting polarizing feedback from his clients. On the one hand, some would say, "Isaac is the best consultant we've ever worked with," which was saying a lot, considering these clients had worked with many other consultants. Often, these were long-term projects where he would spend a year or two with them, and they seemed to genuinely love him. If his business year was filled with these kinds of projects, he always got feedback that he was a "rock star."

On the other hand, Isaac would have shorter-term projects, six weeks to six months, and these clients were more likely to describe him as verbose, unclear, and slow to respond, and they'd say that he appeared overwhelmed. If he had a year filled with these shorter-term projects, the feedback he received was abysmal—and there seemed to be no in-between.

When this came to light in his performance review, it really scared him. Frankly, he was terrified of losing his job and being forced into retirement. This felt like a nightmare for him since he loves his work so much. He reached out to me and said, "I don't know why I'm getting this feedback because I'm clearly the most experienced consultant in the firm." He was pushing back against the client feedback, blaming them, essentially saying, "The clients who don't appreciate me are unsophisticated, they lack proper processes, their products are not competitive," and so on.

Isaac's great strength was being able to dig into market data, financial data, and all kinds of other data sources —at a level of detail that would exhaust most people—and uncover opportunities to make a real impact for the client. What we discovered in the impact statements, however, was that he didn't always bring people along with him in this process, preferring to work in a vacuum.

Because of how deep he would dive into things and his confidence in his intellect, he wouldn't tell others what he was doing or bring them along via regular updates. If pressed for an update, he would confuse the client with his depth. Also, he wasn't sufficiently considering their input, hypotheses, or ideas. For him, the work was an individual academic exercise and began with the false assumption that "My intellect is all that matters."

This seemed reasonable in Isaac's mental operation system from several standpoints. For one, this is where he had found success time and time again—using his intellect to serve the client. For another thing, he could easily justify his assumption by insisting, "This is what they're paying me for—to use my intellect to help them out."

Finally, he justified his assumption because experience had taught him how clients often had the wrong instincts about how to solve their problems. After all, isn't that why they hired him in the first place? This assumption blinded him to the fact that, at the end of the day, the clients were still the leaders of the company. As such, they deserved the respect to share their thoughts and be informed of the progress—even when his insights truly were better. This evolved into intellectual arrogance disguised by an additional false assumption: "This is a short project where I have to produce results, so I don't have time to waste listening to their bad ideas."

This meant he would be deep in the data for several weeks, never communicating what he was doing, never sending an update or asking them questions, and the clients would get agitated. For instance, the CEO might ask, "Isaac, what are your early thoughts here?" To which he would respond, "I don't know. I'm still too deep in the data."

This wasn't because he didn't actually know anything yet. It was because he personally didn't want to put his name to anything that he wasn't 100 percent behind. In his own way, he felt he was protecting the clients by not sharing early insights. Past experience had taught him how sharing too much too early could sometimes sabotage the process if clients chose to act upon incomplete information. Therefore, he would avoid updating them about what he was doing or invite them to make their own hypothesis because he genuinely believed it was best for them.

When I interviewed the clients and colleagues who were a part of his best client experiences, I pressed them to answer, "Did Isaac show up differently with you?" They confirmed they were big fans because of the quality of his output—but the experience of working with him was similar to his detractors.

It seemed that working in a vacuum wasn't just some accidental by-product of his blind spot—it had become an intentional part of his strategy being driven by his false assumptions. He admitted to me that he didn't prioritize ongoing communication with the client because he falsely assumed the quality of his findings would fill in any gaps of client rapport and carry the weight of influence. His assumption was "Whatever stress or agitation I may have caused by my noncommunication would be forgiven by the brilliance of my final answer."

One of the stakeholders shared the following:

> *"Isaac is very focused on being accurate and has great attention to detail... and yet often the client context requires more practical, rapid, and 'mostly right' direction and action."*

Instead, Isaac was only seeing things through his own perspective, his false assumptions blinding him to the perspective of the clients he was serving.

After six weeks of no communication, Isaac would then pop up to the surface as if to say, "Ta-da! Look, I solved all your problems!" Too often, the solution he presented would be difficult for the C-suite to understand since they had no information about how he arrived at his conclusions. He would present a ninety-page deck filled with data and insights they couldn't understand because he hadn't brought them along and synthesized it for them. Additionally, many of the impact statements showed his explanations could become muddled or fail to clearly connect the analysis to actionable insights.

At this point, the greatest and most damaging false assumption he was making was "As long as I get the right answer, that's all that matters—whether they understand it or not."

This false assumption perpetuated behaviours that were irritating for his clients. It blocked them from hearing Isaac's solution, since they felt alienated by his process. Not only did they not take the time to understand the solution—they wanted to make him *wrong.* The negative experience of his noncommunication caused them to make their own false assumptions about him: "This guy doesn't care about us. If he knew what he was really doing, he would have informed us along the way. There's no way this can be right."

Ultimately, this led to the clients testing him because they didn't like being excluded from his process. They would question his analysis and findings, causing Isaac to become defensive and resistant. I'm simplifying things here, but his responses to them would become unempathetic: "Well, if you don't get it, you are obviously not capable of executing on the solution I worked so hard to provide."

As you can see, it was messy, to say the very least.

We worked together for around twelve months to process through all these false assumptions and help untangle them from his way of thinking. This was a challenge because Intellects like Isaac can easily use their intelligence to justify their way of doing things—especially when it worked for them in the past.

It's been a couple years since I worked with Isaac, but he now regularly receives positive reviews from his clients. His leadership team has always considered him to be an invaluable asset to their team, but the changes he's made in his collaboration style enabled him to be consistently successful on his projects and add even more value. By recognizing his false assumptions, he is better able to adapt his style and work more effectively with a wide variety of clients and colleagues.

As a result, not only are his clients and leadership team happier, but Isaac himself is also happier in his work and confident he won't be forced into retirement. He can continue to contribute his intellect as a consultant as long as he likes.

He still calls me on an ad hoc basis to talk through situations. "I need to give the client an update," he'll say to me. "I need to figure out what message to give them since I don't have a complete answer yet." In my mind, this is incredible progress because it shows how he has overcome the false assumptions that plagued him. He's been able to replace them with a better understanding of the importance of including the client in the process and the powerful impact this has on their experience of working with him. All with just a little bit of clear and more frequent communication.

 ## Alison: The Advocate

For our final case study on false assumptions, it's time to meet Alison. While her background was in financial services, Alison had risen through the ranks incredibly fast in her company's technology practice, making partner in almost half the time it normally takes. Not only was she smart and hardworking, but she was exceptionally skilled in developing client rapport and in business development by advocating for her clients' needs. In particular, she has proven herself to be adept at understanding digital strategy and is an expert in the emerging field of artificial intelligence and how it can be used in the intersection of technology, marketing, and customer experience.

Everyone at the company raved about the quality of her client relationships. She bonded with them by going to bat to get the best delivery team for them. Then she'd work tirelessly with the team to maintain the highest possible quality during the execution. Add all this together, and it's easy to see why she was promoted so quickly, but maybe you can also see why I've nicknamed her the "Advocate."

Her great strength is her ability to connect with clients, to partner with them by heading out into the unknown, and not only solve problems but fight for them within her organization to provide the experts and outstanding services they need to conquer their challenges. She is also great at challenging the thinking of her clients by bringing in new ideas to help them look at their work in a new light to achieve the outcomes they want.

Unfortunately, her impact statements also revealed how this spirit of advocacy could sometimes manifest itself in a way that created conflict when she felt like coworkers were not supporting her. She could become critical of others when they didn't exactly align with her way of thinking. This can happen when someone's mind takes on an assumption that becomes a filter through which they see everything else. If the filter is set to "friend or foe" and defaults to "foe," then all of one's focus can unconsciously see enemies everywhere.

For Alison, this showed up most often on internal issues she was personally passionate about, such as addressing gender bias and equity. Her advocacy for this cause was further bolstered because she noticed how her clients' executive teams were reasonably equitable—maybe 40 to 50 percent representation of women among the group. Yet when she was with her internal team at work, she was often the only woman in the room. As an advocate for clients *and* for equity, she saw this as a problem. "We should look like our clients," she thought, "so why don't we? When our clients look at our leadership team, why aren't they seeing this equity represented here?"

Here's the thing: she wasn't wrong about this line of thinking. Her company claimed to want an equitable and diverse workforce, so as an advocate for gender equity, she was right to point this out and ask what was being done about it. This became a problem, however, when it became the filter through which she saw everything.

She would go to a meeting, and everything would seem fine throughout. Then at the end of the meeting, she would pull the leader aside and proceed to pick apart every little thing he had said, which could possibly be interpreted as gender bias. Rather than this being constructive criticism, however, it would be a full-fledged personal attack—to the point of leaving him feeling awful about himself.

Don't get me wrong. I'm a huge advocate for equity and inclusion, but her approach was taken to the extreme, where it was unhealthy and unhelpful. None of the other females in the meeting would have issues with the way the male leader had said things—they knew he was well-intentioned, and if he used the pronouns "he/him" with more regularity than "she/her" or "they/them," it wasn't out of any ill will toward diversity. Yet Alison assumed she could best fight this perceived injustice by criticizing anything and everything he had said.

She didn't realize how she was injecting bias into situations where none existed. Even I experienced a similar overreaction from her once when she sent me an article featuring her so I could provide feedback. When I responded, I wrote, "The article is great; it really shows your expertise. I did notice, though, that your headshot makes you look a little casual. You might want to consider an updated, more professional one." And then I sent her an example—a headshot of her company's CEO, who *also* happened to be a woman.

Alison's response to me was, "You would never say this to a guy," accusing my comment of being gender-biased, which was a false assumption about me. I didn't mind, but I could see how her approach might have been better received if she had asked me a question like "Do you think your feedback might be gender-biased?" rather than jumping to the conclusion that I was biased.

I replied to her honestly, saying, "I often say the same thing to guys!" But with her ultra-Advocate filter engaged, she felt compelled to argue with me over the headshot. She's a busy person, yet she took the time to send me multiple emails back and forth over this. Why? Maybe because she wanted to change *me* so I would never tell another woman she should update her headshot in the future? Her false assumptions about what was worth fighting for made her completely blind to my positive intention to help her.

Other examples of her proclivity to criticize and tear others down came out in the impact statements. For instance, if she attended a work event organized by someone else, she would spend her time detailing aloud what was wrong with the event and speak poorly about whoever organized it. As one stakeholder put it, "Alison seems to view her peers as competition as opposed to collaborators. That's why she doesn't miss an opportunity to point out their flaws."

Underpinning all of this were a number of false assumptions, but the biggest two for her were the linked ideas of "I can say anything I want when I feel strongly about something" and "It's my duty to point out the flaws in others. Nothing will change unless I always advocate."

At least in part, these false assumptions seemed to have come about as a defence mechanism. Like many people who are promoted quickly, she had endured high scrutiny from others watching her quick ascent. Others had certainly talked behind *her* back, wondering, "What's so great about her? Why is she getting all this attention?" When combined with the gender inequity among senior leaders, this seemed to have made her more sensitive in a way where she would then overreact to any type of pain or perceived injustice she saw in the workplace.

I coach leaders like Alison to accept that this scrutiny is to be expected given people's reaction to her accelerated career path, similar to how a celebrity has to accept the paparazzi following them around. No one is saying it's fair—it's just the price of fame. Likewise, becoming "famous" in the workplace would also invite some jealous curiosity. Rather than be pragmatic about this and brush it off, Alison felt attacked.

Now, she could have said to herself, "You know what? I'm going to take this scrutiny and curiosity and use my strengths to show the positive things I can do and bring up others along with me." That in itself would have been *positive* advocacy.

Instead, she had adopted another false assumption and then ran with it: "People are judging me, so I have to take them down to elevate myself." This is the negative aspect of the Advocate because they can feel like they have to fight everyone in order to protect their interests and the interests of their teams. Alison's assumptions of attack meant she couldn't see the truth in someone's feedback or even interpret their comments as opinions—she could only see things through the lens of a fight to be won.

A fascinating aspect of Alison's story, different from the other two, is that it shows how false assumptions can be acquired. From the impact statements gathered, it didn't appear she had always been like this. One stakeholder even observed that he believed she had taken on some of this negativity from a previous supervisor who had been known as a bully in the company. False assumptions can be formed through our learned experiences, which actually make them feel more legitimate.

A distinct marker of Advocates is that they will *passionately* fight for what they believe in. This can make an incredibly positive impact when done in the spirit of collaboration, but it can also create a toxic and hostile work environment when done in the spirit of negativity.

This is exactly what had happened with Alison—her negative energy had created a toxic culture around her. When HR investigated some complaints about her conduct, they found polarizing views of Alison: some people thought she walked on water—and others felt like she was walking all over *them*.

Another interesting outcome from the stakeholder impact statements was discovering just how much Alison needed validation from others. Based on some descriptions of how she would tear others down, you would think she didn't care much about what others thought of her. In reality, though, the root of her false assumptions was her own personal insecurity. One stakeholder hit this on the head when they observed: "She sets a high aspiration for herself and what she deems as her integrity, but she forgets that people are human and imperfect actions or behaviours will happen."

With her need to validate her own worth and value, she latched on to the mistakes of others, no matter how small, and became fixated to the point of losing focus on what was truly important. For Alison, this meant she had developed blind spots where she didn't care about the relationship damage that could result from her comments to peers.

Working with her through these issues was complex because no one wanted Alison to lose the overwhelmingly positive aspects of the Advocate which had made her successful. It was a combination of helping her learn to pick her battles and seek to understand others' actions and words before criticizing them. She had to learn to assume *positive* intentions in others and then calm herself before addressing others.

Advocates often present a tough exterior, but when I've presented this feedback to them, they often break down when they realize how harsh they have been on others. Underneath the armor, they tend to be sensitive individuals, which is no different with Alison. As a result, she committed that through our coaching, she would clear out all the closets full of skeletons in her professional relationships. How? She chose to appreciate the efforts of others rather than fixate on their mistakes—and simultaneously took a hard look at her own faults to fix them.

She's also made strides in proactively *asking* for feedback rather than assuming it's her job to *give* feedback. She has learned to be less self-oriented and more others-aware, considering how the other person will receive her feedback first and questioning whether the feedback is necessary.

For example, she once called me and said, "I need to tell this person they screwed up." I responded, "Are you sure you have to? Have they asked you for feedback?" It turned out the individual in question didn't even work in the same group as her, so she *absolutely* did not have to intervene.

The fact that she called me made me happy, though. It showed me she's learned to recognize when she's about to step over the edge and do damage. Over the course of our work, Alison learned not to assume she owns the absolute truth but to be open to hearing the other side of the story. For example, before she gives feedback, she now has the skillset to first say, "I know this wasn't your intention. Here is what I think I observed, but what are your thoughts?"

Alison learned to see how her false assumptions were damaging her relationships with her coworkers and how she didn't always need to start a fight. There were often other team members who could more appropriately intervene. Additionally, she learned she could positively contribute to gender equity by advocating for female talent on her team. She could also encourage, support, and celebrate HR and other leaders' initiatives aimed at correcting gender disparity. Most importantly, she could be an advocate for important issues without damaging relationships by appointing herself as the judge, jury, and enforcement officer.

As a result of this new awareness, Alison was able to refocus her energy and double down on her impact through her projects, contribution of ideas, and speaking. She focused on elevating herself by pulling people *up* with her instead of looking for opportunities to tear people down. She changed her lens from seeing everything in black-and-white to understanding there are more shades she can use to make the world a brighter place.

Alison admits that although the impact statements were hard for her to hear, it led her to make changes that helped her have her best year ever. She improved the quality of all her relationships, and because she was less focused on what everyone else was doing wrong, she focused more on what they could do right together. She is happier, more confident, more focused on her goals, and able to contribute to a positive environment while being unburdened by problems that are not hers alone to solve.

The Takeaway

It's likely you've run into at least one or all of these versions of false assumptions in your team or collaborations. Conflict can serve as a compass directing you toward identifying some false assumptions. Are there assumptions in your own "operating system" you may need to take a fresh look at?

Regardless of how they show up, false assumptions are one of the most damaging of the blind spots because of how deceptive they are. When they go unchecked, they easily become a breeding ground for more blind spots.

With David, we saw how false assumptions can often be tied to our strengths, making it easy to justify them rather than deal with them. With Isaac, we saw how his false assumptions fed into a different view of success from the clients he was serving, which created their own false assumptions about him. And in Alison's story, her false assumptions were causing an unhealthy detachment from the feelings of others.

To some degree, all three had to recognize how their false assumptions were leading them to overindex their own emotions, creating a negative impact on other people, and by extension, on the business itself.

In our next blind spot, we're going to take a deep dive into unhealthy detachment from the emotions of others and the toll it takes on individuals, work culture, and even on the bottom line.

But we'll also address how this can be solved by increasing our *self*-awareness through becoming even more *others*-aware.

Summary

How false assumptions happen:	Your brain has formed false assumptions based on past experiences that seem similar to your current situation.
The shift you need:	Make your subconscious assumptions *conscious* to validate or challenge them.
Self-reflection questions to help you uncover false assumptions:	• What past experiences do I think are most similar to my current role, project, or other challenge I am facing? • What expectations or approaches am I assuming to be correct but have not confirmed with others? • What assumptions might I need to validate (about our culture, about our people, about our clients)? • Who do I need to ask to validate or debunk these assumptions?

YOUR NOTES

....

....

....

....

....

....

....

....

....

....

....

....

....

....

UNHEALTHY DETACHMENT

Simple definition:	Things people do or ways they behave when they fail to prioritize what's important to others.
Root cause:	People's behaviours create conflict and frustration because they are undervaluing the emotions and priorities of other people.
Often results in:	Confusion, disconnection, inaccessibility.

We've all heard the phrase "It's not personal; it's business." Maybe we've been guilty of using it ourselves. But great leaders seem to understand how driving business forward requires them to build personal connections with others. "Personal" and "business" don't exist in separate boxes, although we sometimes pretend they do!

As leaders, we spend a lot of time thinking about our mission, our vision, and creating calls to action for others because these are important drivers of success. Despite this, I've noticed many leaders tend to overlook the role human emotions play in either optimizing or deteriorating the work environment. Perhaps it is the longstanding notion that when you come to work, you need to "check your feelings at the door." But if we're honest enough with ourselves, very few of us actually do this—myself included. So why do we expect others to?

A greater challenge is how to *uncover* the feelings someone has about their work—or more importantly, those they work with. Most of us keep our feelings hidden and justify it by thinking, *I don't have to like them. I just need to work with them.* But the degree to which we are emotionally connected to each other, and the purpose of our organizations *does* fuel our motivation to do our best work.

This is why it is important to recognize the link between our emotional intensity and how attached or detached we are to circumstances, events, and people—in both personal and professional contexts. The right amount of attachment creates the ideal conditions for your performance, while *too much* attachment brings its own issues in terms of stress and control. This second area of blind spots is a form of *unhealthy detachment*, specifically an unhealthy detachment from the emotions of others.

Rather than believing the "check our feelings at the door" mentality is a reasonable approach, most great leaders recognize the critical role emotions play in how we set others up for success—and set ourselves up for success too, for that matter. This doesn't mean you have to go out and earn a PhD in psychology or gather the team in a weekly session of singing "Kumbaya." What it means is gaining the awareness that when there is an unhealthy detachment from the emotions of others, it does far more than just create a "bad vibe." It is directly connected to a misalignment in how success itself is viewed.

In my book *Work Smart*, I discussed a topic I want to revisit here: the idea that success in the workplace often depends on transcending self-awareness to gain more *others-awareness.*

That's not to say being self-aware isn't important—on the contrary, it's incredibly important! Later, we'll even dive into the blind spot of unconscious habits, a form of professional self-sabotage resulting from poor self-awareness. But often what I've found in coaching people through this particular blind spot of unhealthy detachment is that they tend to be *very* self-aware with their own emotions. Where things break down is when they are painfully *unaware* of their impact on the emotions of others—widening the gap between their intentions and impact.

We've all heard of the Golden Rule: "Do unto others as you would have them do unto you." But the best leaders understand that we need to upgrade this rule as we upgrade our own mental operating systems. We need to move away from treating others the way *we* want to be treated (that is, self-awareness) and into treating others the way *they* want to be treated, which is true others-awareness.

To have a proper understanding of unhealthy detachment, it helps to recognize its place in a spectrum of how we prioritize aspects of our work. There is also such a thing as *healthy detachment, unhealthy attachment,* and *healthy attachment.*

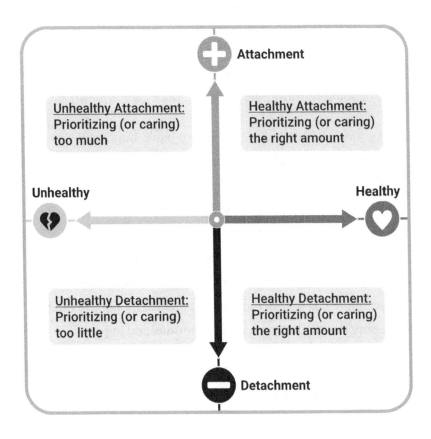

When we place a low priority on low-importance issues, this is *healthy detachment.* These are low-impact issues, not worth battling over. However, when we care too much about low-importance issues, we display an *unhealthy attachment* to those issues.

Likewise, when we place a high priority on high-importance issues, we have a healthy attachment. If we set a low priority for high-importance issues, we can label it as an unhealthy detachment.

Where you feel stressed it could be a sign of unhealthy detachment or unhealthy attachment. Often there is a direct relationship between an unhealthy detachment and a related unhealthy attachment.

For example, you may have an unhealthy attachment to alcohol consumption after a tough day, which could signal an unhealthy detachment from taking care of your health. In the examples provided in the client stories, we're going to focus primarily on unhealthy detachments, understanding there is likely a related unhealthy attachment lurking. This often manifests as a blind spot.

In my experience with witnessing unhealthy detachments and their impact on collaborations, there are two ways they cause damage as a blind spot. First, people can exhibit behaviours that create disconnection with their colleagues due to a general lack of understanding of how their colleagues feel. Second, unhealthy detachment can also lead a person's colleagues to assume there is a lack of empathy—they believe their colleague *knows* how they feel but simply chooses *not* to care. One is a connection problem, and the other is an empathy problem. Both are unhealthy, and it can get really messy when the two become linked.

As we did with false assumptions, we'll look at three versions of how unhealthy detachment caused blind spots for both individuals and organizations. In fact, we already saw with false assumptions how some unhealthy detachments can develop. There's a chance some of these may hit a little too close to home. Still, it's helpful to ask, what similar situations have you encountered within your own organization—and how did they end up?

 ## Patrick: The Peacemaker

Fair warning, this one doesn't have a happy ending, but it serves to remind us just how damaging these blind spots can actually be when they are left in the dark.

Patrick had been CEO for a little under a year when I first met with him. Since he was an external hire and new to the organization, the board had invested in helping him acclimate to the company by creating an action plan with specific KPIs, assigning him a mentor, a coach, and governance training for him and the executive team. The former CEO had been quite divisive and had created lots of conflict, so the selection committee appreciated Patrick's track record of forming strong collaborations and his ability to drive cultural transformations. According to his coach at the time, Patrick scored off the charts in the areas of empathy and collaboration—and I saw the same strong qualities when I worked with him.

Following a turbulent time for the company, Patrick happily embraced his role as a Peacemaker and was committed to creating a work environment free of conflict. It was his personal goal to be there for his team and ensure they felt heard. His collaborative spirit and vision for a consensus-driven team came from a well-intentioned space.

When gathering contextual comments and general appreciation feedback from his team, Patrick was described as a genuinely nice person—and people saw that he had great intentions. As you've seen in our discussion already, this isn't always the case, so having a team who saw his intentions put him in a good starting point to succeed. Furthermore, being a Peacemaker helped him to earn the admiration, confidence, and general trust of the people he worked with daily. I could immediately feel his genuine kindness when we began working together.

So why was I called in by this board to work with a CEO who was such an empathetic collaborator?

As a Peacemaker, Patrick enjoyed working hard to prove he was a nice person. He traveled across the country, connecting with employees, and was particularly popular with junior talent. After one visit, he even received a poem from the customer service group because of how much they enjoyed his visit. How many CEOs do you know whose employees write nice poems for them? With these tokens of affection, Patrick prided himself on the cultural turnaround he was making, and in his mind, he only had a sea of happy fans behind him.

However, the downside many Peacemakers face is a tendency to sidestep *any* conflict rather than look for ways to *resolve* conflict. This was Patrick's go-to approach for keeping the peace. For better or worse, managing conflict is necessary for growth, both on a personal and business level. But Patrick just flat-out avoided it at all costs.

As things progressed, the board noted Patrick was not delivering in his primary responsibilities as CEO. The role demanded strategy development, problem-solving with a quick turnaround time, and an efficient level of managing real-time issues—not just likability. Yet Patrick was so focused on the appearance of conflict-free collaboration that it came across as him dragging his feet on decision-making.

And it wasn't just the board who felt this way. Although his team liked Patrick as a person, they also experienced his foot-dragging. In reality, they felt he would take chunks of time listening to what they had to say and completely ignore their input when it came time to make a decision.

For example, a team meeting would end, and they would be left with more questions than answers, wondering what action was actually going to be taken from the discussion. Without clear communication on which action would be taken or setting a deadline for the action, Patrick was creating an unhealthy detachment from their needs. He believed he was keeping his team from conflict. Meanwhile, their heads were spinning, ultimately causing them frustration. All his goodwill as a nice person evolved into distrust from his team members.

Being a Peacemaker as a leader has its place in business. Teams appreciate someone who can think on their feet and de-stress everyone by stepping up and handling situations that arise when tensions are high. But Patrick seemed to have adopted a philosophy of "good vibes only" and chose to ignore any issues that didn't immediately translate into positive feedback for him. In this way, he created an emotional divide between himself and the board and between himself and the team he believed loved him.

The impact statements also revealed that Patrick had a tendency to be people-pleasing in groups but more passive-aggressive with individuals:

"He needs to find a way to set boundaries, stand up for his interests, push back, and handle conflict. He is too inclusive and is trying hard to make everyone happy. He is more

conflict-averse in a group; he is more confronting one-on-one, but then inconsistent later."

As you can imagine, this inconsistency only added to the frustration his team was feeling.

When confronted with this information, he immediately felt angry and betrayed by his management team. Seeing in writing that they liked him as a person but had misgivings about his effectiveness as a leader blindsided Patrick. He was particularly taken aback by their suggestions of how he could improve. He felt this was a step too far.

From his perspective, the team was happy with his performance. Blinded by his role as a Peacemaker, he truly believed he had great working relationships with them and that the board members were the only people who were "against" him. His self-awareness had led him to believe he was more attached to others than he truly was, but the feedback showed he had difficulty tapping into others-awareness.

This inability to understand his team's true feelings, even when spelled out on a page, created a disconnect on multiple levels. Hence, the unhealthy-detachment blind spot brought out his own frustration and heightened his sense of "me versus the board."

This came to a head when the board reviewed the findings from the impact statements. They asked him to go through coaching with me for a season to work through the development areas that were identified. He felt betrayed and set up. When the board suggested he rebuild his self-confidence to earn the board and team's trust in decision-making, he interpreted the suggestion as an attack from the enemy. Rather than embrace a chance to grow and improve, Patrick declined.

This was yet another damaging aspect of his blind spot—he couldn't see how the board actually cared about his success and wanted to find a way to work together effectively. After all, they had picked him for the job because of his strengths and had verbalized that their intentions were to help him become the leader they felt he could be.

Ironically, they were actually trying to be Peacemakers to him, but by this point, he couldn't see this. Ultimately, his unhealthy attachment to his own emotions, combined with his unhealthy detachment from their feelings, launched his brain into fight-or-flight mode, taking offense to their input.

I warned you this wouldn't have a happy ending. It would be great to say Patrick was able to take a step back, reflect on the feedback, embrace growth, and thrive as the CEO of the company over time.

But I can't.

He told the board he preferred to continue working with his own coach. Since she was focusing on his strengths, he believed this was the best way for him to elevate his performance. The irony is that I also have my clients focus on their strengths, but as a method to address opportunities for improvement, not to ignore problems until they fester. Overly focusing on his strengths became its own blind spot, compounding his other blind spots to Patrick's detriment.

Instead of putting his passion into the things that mattered most to the board and his team, Patrick allowed his Peacemaker tendencies to get the better of him. He chose to ignore the feedback, assuming it was just unfair scrutiny, and the conflict with the board continued. He simply would not see things from their perspective.

I only had four sessions with Patrick to review the stakeholder interviews. As I wrapped up my last meeting with him, I said goodbye and wished him well, feeling disappointed I wouldn't have the opportunity to work with him further. I was hopeful, though, since I respect my clients' decisions on who can best help them and was willing to accept that maybe I wasn't the right fit for him.

In a show of good faith in Patrick's desire to work with his own coach, the board gave him six more months to keep working with her and prove he could be the leader the company needed. Unfortunately, when the six months concluded, there had been no improvement, and he was let go and replaced with an interim leader.

Do I think Patrick was an incompetent CEO? Not at all.

I wish I could have had more time with him. We could have aimed his natural affinity for people at the board members' feedback and taken a deep dive into ways he could demonstrate and improve his decision-making process. He and the board were actually aligned with many of their intentions, but his unhealthy detachment from their expressed needs kept him from acting on them.

By choosing to avoid conflict at all costs, Patrick was unwilling to look for and work through his blind spot. He believed being an advocate for "peace" within his team created a close attachment between them, but it actually had the reverse effect. They had felt more exasperation than peace, growing more frustrated meeting after meeting.

Rather than having tough conversations and closing the gaps between his performance and his potential, he buried himself in his blind spot. Simply put, he couldn't make peace with becoming the leader the board, his team, and the corporation needed him to be.

I will never know if my work with him would have yielded a different result, but I do know that we would have developed a plan to internalize the feedback and help him move forward as a true Peacemaker. We could have worked through the emotional turmoil so he could experiment with new ways of collaborating with the board and his team. It's possible that his overwhelming feelings of betrayal overshadowed his ability to consider the feelings of those around him. It ultimately caused so much space between him and the board that it cost him his job—a job he loved.

The ability to empathize and consciously read the room is a skill that takes time and effort for anyone to master. It takes serious dedication to be able to look past what you *want* to see and find opportunities for growth. It takes time to explore ways to close the gaps between reality and your vision for your team.

I always encourage my clients to take some time to consciously notice what's happening around them at work—the good *and* the not-so-good. How are people receiving them? How are others engaging with them? When making a presentation, I encourage them to consider everyone's reactions to what they're saying—and then ask how they feel.

As leaders, if we're going to ask how people feel, there has to be a willingness to receive honest feedback—and take it in by flexing our empathy muscles before reacting. We have to be unafraid to self-correct based on the input we receive, even if it leads to conflict. After all, a true Peacemaker *makes peace* where there is conflict and uses it as an opportunity to create strength.

Gary: The Guardian

Gary was one of the core members of the executive team as the chief legal officer for a large investment agency. When I first met him, he had been there for almost twelve years, and the new CEO was looking to support Gary during many constructive changes to the organizational structure and Gary's team. Gary had a deep-seated intention to take great care of his team, which is how he got his nickname "The Guardian."

If this sounds like a stretch, it's not. Multiple stakeholders among the leadership would say things like, "He's saved the company many, many times." He consistently took on high-risk work that required him to unwind complexity and effectively negotiate the company out of precarious deals that had gone south. Not only had he rescued the company more times than they could count, but he'd also helped them avoid other dangerous situations. He was especially gifted at identifying risks and fearless in untangling the difficulties no one else wanted to touch.

Where many lawyers just offered advice and let the business take all the risk, he showed he was willing to take the brunt of a difficult scenario and navigate the company to safety. Because of this, the leadership was confident they could count on him to save them from trouble—or, better yet, keep them *out* of trouble.

Gary took a similar Guardian-like approach with his team. He was always working tirelessly to look out for others. He wanted his team members to feel safe and secure in their roles without being overwhelmed or burned out. However, looking out for the well-being of his team showed up as an unhealthy attachment when Gary merged his Guardian role with his own false assumptions of what was actually best for his team.

Gary learned from the stakeholder interviews how mistaken he was about the best way to protect his team members. Rather than having a conversation about delegating responsibilities or offering them new opportunities, he'd speak on their behalf with comments like "They're busy on deals; they're not interested in this stuff." Or "People don't want this kind of work."

The Guardian role was so embedded within Gary that if a team member asked about taking on more work or even a different role, he'd respond, "That's not really what you want!" Even though they'd just said that they wanted it. As you can imagine, this type of "protection" wasn't creating the kind of work environment Gary intended, and it became frustrating for his team members.

One of the stakeholders mentioned that Gary had no structure in place to help team members develop into new roles within the agency. As a result, people would simply leave to pursue new opportunities elsewhere. The agency was losing talented people, and their initial employee engagement scores were low. Gary's team was chronically understaffed, causing everyone to have more than their fair share of work—which only made Gary more overloaded and unavailable to respond to urgent requests from his team properly.

He had tons of knowledge to bring to the table from his days as a deal lawyer, but stakeholders pointed to multiple examples where his level of experience would backfire in meetings. Gary would get caught up on a detail, and the team would feel as though they had wasted time listening to his opinion on this one point rather than getting his input on the more critical items.

The perception developing around Gary was "He's a micromanager." A micromanager who also had a rather threatening sense of humor. His team referred to one running joke where Gary would say, "Well, if you do that, you might as well leave your business cards on the table." What Gary considered a light-hearted joke was not only unappreciated by his team, but they felt *offended* because they were highly competent and professional lawyers working hard to do their best. For them, it wasn't a laughing matter, and this was just one example of how Gary was detached from their true feelings.

When Gary was in work mode, his *modus operandi* was to stay objective and make the plays necessary to seal the deal, even though he was supposed to facilitate meetings with deal lawyers rather than doing their job. With all this happening, his team members felt overworked, undervalued, and as though he may fire any of them at any time.

Meanwhile, Gary the Guardian truly believed he was protecting his team members from unnecessary and unwanted opportunities. This unhealthy detachment kept him in a mode where he kept dismissing the thought of delegating opportunities and ignoring his team's requests for career growth.

One stakeholder addressed his Guardian nature by stating:

> *"He is almost too respectful of the fact that his team members are busy, so much so that he is reluctant to ask them for help on the work that he needs to get done."*

Somehow, Gary needed to learn how delegating tasks could be a positive experience for himself and his team members. He needed to see that he wasn't protecting them from overwork— he was creating roadblocks to their success.

Another stakeholder made a keen observation when they said this:

> *"Many people would see working more closely with Gary as an opportunity to learn from him and get some mentorship and guidance in the process. Especially some of the more junior team members might enjoy having more access to him so that it would be a win-win."*

In addition to this, gender-bias issues were emerging in the impact statements from female members of his team. This is a huge blind spot in the workplace right now, and multiple individuals felt he was inadvertently being biased despite the high number of women on his team in the corporate law department.

For one thing, they felt as though he wasn't great at nurturing the talent of women, with one female team member overtly stating, "He doesn't let me show my personality" in her presentations. Gary appeared to have some assumptions about what made a good presentation based on his own core beliefs— and unfortunately, these were being translated as women needing to present more "masculine" if they were to be taken seriously.

Let me be clear: this wasn't his intention at all. As a Guardian, he intended to protect the women on his team from being treated as "less than" by others. But there was a presumption on his part that for the women on his team to sound credible, they had to sound just like *him* in their presentations. Gary's intention to protect them from gender bias at the hands of others backfired in them experiencing gender bias from *him*.

When we began working together, Gary was leading from within a vacuum. He needed a strategy to address the blind spots of his Guardian nature and move into the space of being a *cocreator* with his team. We started by looking at the impact he had on others. Remember others-awareness? That's where the real turnaround began.

One of Gary's revelations in reading the impact statements was finally seeing how his failure to delegate tasks to team members was communicating a lack of trust in them. Reading their true feelings showed him how unattached he had truly been to their desires and how much they recognized the importance of their work. He could now see what his Guardian mentality had blinded him to: they would treat any new opportunities with respect and deliver quality work to him without neglecting their regular responsibilities.

Furthermore, his team members had always thought he cared about them and was a great person, but they didn't get to see enough of this side of him. Too often at work, Gary presented as a stereotypical type A workaholic, which led to some incon- sistency between his messaging and actions.

For example, he told team members to use their vacation time, but he had a way of bragging that he never used any time off for himself. He would tell them to protect their personal time, yet they would receive emails from him whenever he had a thought he wanted to address, no matter the day or time. They were concerned with how frustrated he seemed at work and wanted to help him. He was trying to protect them but not modeling this for himself.

In order to become a cocreator, it was time for him to start opening up to them first. He also had to learn to notice what was important to his team and honour this information with real action.

One of the first concerns we addressed was Gary's need to increase his capacity and reduce the timeline for recruiting new hires. He started to involve his team in recruitment more, which helped everyone. It streamlined the process of onboarding new hires, but it had the added benefit of helping team members feel trusted to share their thoughts on who the best candidates were. By empowering his team, Gary could see how they were able to provide insight and help with recruiting high-quality candidates.

Gary also started modeling for his team the value of taking some time away from work by taking advantage of personal time off (PTO). They loved seeing him use some vacation time to spend with his family or how he would disconnect in *healthy* ways by leaving at six on Tuesdays to take his kids to hockey practices and games. Seeing these glimpses of his personal life only served to make his team feel more emotionally connected to him.

Next, he began talking with his team more about skills development, even going so far as looking into how to enhance people's marketability. He learned how to voice his personal concerns regarding how to provide them with constructive feedback *without* being threatening. When he was open with them, they were genuinely excited to learn from him.

As a Guardian, Gary had always been genuinely concerned about the welfare of his team—and what team member doesn't appreciate a leader who cares about them? But his impact on them hadn't matched his intentions.

He was so used to saying no as a way to protect them until someone asked him to give more yeses than he was used to. Instead of just jumping to the other side of the pendulum and coaching him to say yes to every new idea coming his way, we shifted into a more balanced space that would allow him to grow into a new kind of leader.

His role as a Guardian has evolved by teaching others how to guard their interests and obtain the skills *they* desire to grow into new positions. As a result, the agency's engagement scores have never been higher, and I'm truly proud of his efforts!

So many clients have worried that if they shift their focus from strategy and the bottom line to making meaningful connections with their team members, they'll lose the edge that gave them their leadership position in the first place. But I've found the opposite to be true—connection with their team helps them gain the followership necessary to be a great leader. Besides, the skills that get someone into a leadership role don't just evaporate when they decide to connect with their team emotionally. Instead of losing skills, they gain a *new* skill.

 Speaking of which, learning how to delegate and how to scale and leverage one's strengths is one of the most desired skills among the boards and CEOs I know. They want to see these qualities because the inability to delegate, scale, and leverage is often a limiting factor to a leader's success. Granted, it's a real challenge to let go when they're accustomed to doing most things themselves as part of their personal success.

If we only stress delegation, we're only halfway there though. Leaders need to *elevate* people to effectively delegate. It's one thing to say you're going to give other people more work; it's another thing to help them emotionally *connect* to that work. To do this, people need to feel empowered, excited, and engaged in order to take ownership of a new opportunity and grow.

 ## Victoria: The Visionary

As a thought leader in her space, Victoria is the author of several books, a highly sought-after speaker, and the CEO of a portfolio of businesses, all within the online learning community. As a Visionary, she has big dreams to revolutionize her industry—and frankly, her vision is often contagious, which is why she started a mentorship program to inspire others to pursue their dreams.

Many of Victoria's team members worked with her as their mentor and were so inspired by her passion and vision, they applied to work with her at her company. Her husband believes in her message so much that he became an executive team member to help support her dream.

In the impact statements, her stakeholders all noted how extremely capable Victoria was at seeing the big picture. She's the type who thrives being onstage, clearly fulfilled by the opportunity of teaching a captivated audience. Beyond her dynamic personality onstage, people described her as a stabilizing and calming force during challenging times. She could create a sense of trust and faith for the team so that even when circumstances were less than ideal, there was a plan in place, and everything would work out.

At this point, though, you're probably wondering, "Yeah, but what's wrong with her?"

Unfortunately, there was a noticeable difference between the "sage on the stage" and the CEO of the company. The company experienced high turnover from team members who struggled with burnout and reported feeling sad, undervalued, and emotionally abused by someone who they had admired and once looked up to.

Like most Visionaries, Victoria was known to set extremely high standards for herself and the company. Nothing wrong with that in and of itself, but many of her team members felt confused and disoriented due to ever-changing creative solutions she was developing for revolutionizing the industry.

A common concern among the stakeholders was that they never did the same thing twice. As team members worked hard to master a concept, it would morph into something else, and a new set of expectations would emerge. If they struggled the first time, there typically wasn't a second chance to iterate and improve because the *next* big thing was already being introduced. In short, too many changes happening too quickly created additional layers of confusion and complexity to their daily work.

At best, Victoria appeared completely oblivious to these feelings. At worst, she appeared indifferent. In the end, you could summarize her unhealthy detachment as "If only people were better at their jobs, our company would achieve my vision."

Her Visionary mindset had made her great at elevating herself and anyone who chose to work with her. But when team members struggled with completing tasks or seemed to fall short of her lofty expectations, they weren't met with understanding. They were met with derision.

Victoria was famous around the offices for saying things like "It's not that hard. I don't understand how something that would take me ten minutes is taking you three hours." Or she would quip, "You're overcomplicating things." One team member recalled a time when Victoria mentioned she could have hired someone else for "much less money" to execute the task with more efficiency than they could. Rather than inspiring her team the way she did an audience, Victoria was creating more stress and burnout with statements displaying a complete disregard for their feelings.

Victoria's approach further eroded the team's performance when she would openly share about a specific person who was struggling. She would actually voice her view that "Joe may not make it" or "may not be a fit." What Victoria didn't realize is how this not only humiliated and demoralized Joe, but it also tainted Joe's credibility with others since everybody knew Victoria was dissatisfied with his performance. As a result, the other team members would either pay less attention to Joe, or they would even openly question his directives. After all, why listen to someone Victoria had effectively described as "on the way out"?

This was not Victoria's intention at all, but many clients I work with don't understand how powerful their words are—powerful at disempowering members of their team. It is hard to say what is more psychologically damaging: the stress of knowing your boss is dissatisfied with your performance and questions whether you can succeed at your job, *or* the humiliation of feeling like everyone is planning for your demise. But these real implications often go unseen by the Visionary.

This can be a common issue with Visionaries because while their ideal world is so clear to them, it simply doesn't imprint into the minds of their team members as easily. When a Visionary is more emotionally attached to the vision than to their people, it becomes really easy to try to force-fit people into the vision. They lose sight of the fact that there has to be a balancing act between remaining connected to the vision and connecting to the efforts of the people entrusted with making the vision a reality. Otherwise, they actually contribute to the eroding of the performance of the individuals they are attempting to inspire.

When we sat down to discuss her feedback, she didn't feel betrayed like Patrick, nor was she as open as Gary. Victoria was *fired up*. She couldn't believe how ungrateful the team members were being. She felt she had worked so hard to get the company to reach new heights, and now these people were tearing her down.

Thankfully, that isn't where Victoria's story ends.

She calmed down after the initial shock of the statements, and our first goal was to work on ways she could become less judgmental of others. For example, she had to learn there was a difference between feeling disappointed over a result and placing judgment and shame on someone over a result. Her unhealthy detachment from the team's emotions had created a massive blind spot—she couldn't see she was creating a work environment *completely* opposite from what she demonstrated in her mentoring program. Not to mention, the constant judgment and harsh criticism wasn't helping her team meet their goals!

Going back into her teaching mindset, Victoria tapped into her others-awareness. By using her empathy to recognize and value their feelings, she started to see how her team needed to be able to count on her for encouragement and support. Once they saw this from her, they could be honest and open about their progress—or lack thereof—without fear of retribution.

Another important aspect of our discussions was helping Victoria open up to ideas and opinions from her team members. This is tough for any Visionary! One practical way she's started doing this is to pay closer attention to how well she treats those who read her books or show up to hear her speak. Then she incorporates those positive behaviours into her own company culture. Since many people on her team were first introduced to her through these other avenues, it's been an easier way for her to realize the discrepancy in how she was treating people—and how she needed to reset and adjust her approach.

Victoria was also the type of Visionary who expected extreme loyalty from others yet didn't seem capable of reciprocating equal loyalty back to her team members. She's had to learn that her level of commitment as a founder and CEO isn't something she should expect her team members to emulate. For example, she would interpret someone taking a vacation as a personal betrayal or an attempt to sabotage the company if it was being taken at an inconvenient time for the business.

One strategy she's implemented to address this particular blind spot is showing more appreciation to others—and appreciating how it's good for team members to take a break from work and come back refreshed, ready to get back to the revolution. She's now consciously looking for ways to thank people or show them they are valued and trusted—which is a huge step for her.

Through these strategies, Victoria is evolving into the positive Visionary she has proven to be *externally* with her audiences by applying those same skills *internally*. As a result, the turnover within her organization has stabilized, and her team is happier and healthier than ever. When she gets triggered by disappointment or a setback and feels her temperature rising, she's learned to take a moment to step back, re-evaluate the situation, and shift to others-awareness.

The Takeaway

I was sitting across from my husband one day when we were both working from home. He couldn't see my screen, but he suddenly interrupted my train of thought and said, "Don't send that email." There was no way he knew what it said or to whom it was addressed, but he knew by the way I was **pounding my fingers on the keyboard** that I was externalizing my negative emotions onto the addressee.

My own personal version of this blind spot was right there on my screen! I knew he was right. This person didn't need to receive my angry email before I properly processed my emotions and did the work to attach to their feelings first. I deleted the angry email and addressed the issue in a much more productive way later.

Patrick, Gary, and Victoria contributed to the unhealthy detachments in their respective companies by overlooking the importance of creating healthy emotional awareness of their team members. Their self-awareness had blinded them from being others-aware.

It's a difficult situation when a leader is consumed by their own emotions and sees constructive criticism as a personal attack. Patrick's unhealthy attachment to his strengths kept him in a state of unhealthy detachment from the important issues the board had raised with him. As a result, he couldn't move out of his perceived sense of victimhood and lost his job.

By facing the false assumptions he had about guarding his team, Gary was able to recognize how his unhealthy attachment to being right was causing an unhealthy detachment from his team's emotions. In return, they now feel valued, and the agency benefits from the success that coincides with happy people who feel heard.

And Victoria is working on taking a step back before assuming her team is trying to hurt her or the business with their mistakes. She's becoming more others-aware in her communication style and involving her team to create a more unified definition of success. By finding the unhealthy attachment she had to her own methods and beliefs, she could develop a healthy attachment to the needs of her team.

As a leader, it's natural to want to maximize your impact by influencing others. Gaining a team's trust requires authentically making those connections that foster followership. Great leaders build strong work relationships by doing the hard work to understand how others feel and making the necessary adjustments along the way.

Time and time again, I've seen how leaders who gain a healthy attachment to the emotions of their team can grow forward and find new roles that bring the light back into their eyes. This kind of excitement tends to be contagious and helps team members feel comfortable sharing about the things that light them up, leading to a more vibrant and productive workplace.

Every leader presented here wanted to be successful, but unhealthy detachment stood in the way. As Victoria's story showed us, sometimes an unhealthy detachment from the emotions of others is rooted in having an overattachment to your personal view of success.

When this happens, it causes misalignment and distrust. In our next blind-spot area, we'll take a deeper dive into this concept of differing views of success and how three leaders got back on track.

Summary

How unhealthy detachments happen:	You are either aware of or ignoring your stakeholders' priorities and emotions, which you are responsible for addressing.
The shift you need:	Realign your efforts to accommodate the key priorities of others...
Self-reflection questions to help you uncover unhealthy detachments:	• What does this role need me to be passionate about? • What do my colleagues and team members need me to be focused on? • What outcomes are most important to others? • Who can help me better understand which priorities have the lowest impact and highest impact?

YOUR NOTES

....

....

....

....

....

....

....

....

....

....

....

....

....

....

....

....

 INTRODUCTION

BLIND SPOTS

 FALSE ASSUMPTIONS

UNHEALTHY DETACHMENT

DIFFERING VIEWS OF SUCCESS

OUTDATED CORE BELIEFS

UNCONSCIOUS HABITS

TRIGGERS FROM PAST PAIN

MISMATCHED MINDSETS

UNCOVERING BLIND SPOTS

CONCLUSION

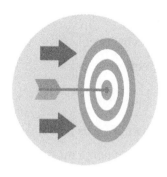

DIFFERING VIEWS
OF SUCCESS

Simple definition:	Things people do or ways they behave because they are focused on different goals.
Root cause:	People's behaviour is influenced by how they have subjectively defined success for themselves and others, which is problematic when there is a failure to create a clear, unified definition of success.
Often results in:	Disengagement, unscalable approaches, collaboration breakdowns

When you think about the word success, what immediately comes to mind?

Many of us begin creating our own ideas of success based on our experiences growing up. For example, maybe your parents rewarded you for achieving accolades in school—money for good grades or loads of affectionate praise. Every time this happened, your brain received a hit of dopamine.

And because dopamine makes us feel good, our brains say, "Hey, that was great! Let's go get some more!" As a result, we continue to seek out dopamine based on what worked in the past. In very little time, this becomes an intrinsic motivator of success, regardless of your individual view of success. In computer terms, it codes your brain with a specific algorithm for how to find success.

For many years, too much of my own "success algorithm" was defined by the job title I held as well as how many promotions and/or how much money I made. The game of getting good grades in school so I could be accepted into prestigious institutions simply transitioned to the game of work. Now it was also about getting *paid well* by *prestigious* companies.

It's normal to be more focused on financial and material goals when we are younger. But as we grow older and wiser, once our needs are met, most of us come to a more holistic definition of success. We start to include in our ambitions aspects like our health, relationships, and making a positive impact in the world.

Whether we are conscious about it or not, our definition of success directs our behaviour and influences how we individually express ourselves. Each of us can point to moments in our lives that validate our personal definitions of success. That's what makes this blind spot tricky for leaders to navigate. When your growth is directly correlated to living out your view of success, leaders experience confusion and conflict when stakeholders call out their perceived strength as a character flaw. For instance, take a leader who prides themselves on their ability to take control and right the ship in any crisis but whose stakeholders point out that the leader is too controlling and difficult to collaborate with.

Consider how everyone's brain is wired to move away from pain and toward pleasure, away from failure and toward success. Each person also has a different lens to look at the world through and individually chooses what success means to them. Thankfully, leaders don't have to solve for everyone in the world, but they do need to solve for their team's view of success. So *how* can leaders find a definition of success that receives the buy-in of an entire team of people?

Most people truly want to be a contributing member of their company. No one wakes up in the morning thinking, *Today's a great day to do a bad job.* They want to feel proud of their work and have positive connections with their coworkers. But a leader's actions are more influential and can have a greater daily impact on a team because of the responsibilities that go with their title. When a leader has difficulty seeing how their view of success clashes with the needs of their team members, the blind spot can actually hinder the effectiveness of the company as a whole.

The "differing views of success" blind spot is so ingrained in our minds that it can be one of the most difficult to change. When our view of success leads us to the next dose of dopamine through raises, praise, and promotions, it solidifies the view into a *fact* within our subconscious. Our mind then becomes laser-focused on moving us toward this view no matter what.

The leaders in our next three case studies wanted to be successful as individuals, which they assumed would then lead their teams and companies to experience the same success. But when their definition of success created a gap between their intentions and impact, they needed an outsider to help them understand their blind spot. They had to learn to reframe their view of success to actually achieve the success they were looking for. We'll see how the desire to be successful went awry for these leaders—and how they were able to get back on track.

 ## Felicia: The Fixer

Felicia's story is one of my favourite transformation stories to share. As the VP of customer engagement in a technology systems implementation company, she was a highly sought-after individual whose clients absolutely loved her. She knew how to put their minds at ease and give them the strategies and tools they needed to deploy complex tech projects when so many others went over budget and over time.

Clients appreciated her confidence and candor in approaching them with a concise and crystal-clear plan in an industry known for its complexities. Felicia spent her days working on the most ambitious projects available and had a real knack for putting out fires—which is why she is dubbed the "Fixer."

She was the epitome of a strong executive presence when working with client teams. Her clear communication skills, mixed with an air of determination, were palpable in meeting rooms. She exuded technical competence and had an obvious passion for getting clients the results they needed. As you can imagine, this made the clients feel safe and cared for.

On any given day, this Fixer knew she was walking into a difficult situation where her clients desperately needed help. Often, tensions were running high, and the room was usually dominated by a mixture of despair, fury, and fear. Sometimes the clients would even consider terminating their agreement with Felicia's consulting company.

As a Fixer, though, Felicia would come in and immediately articulate her diagnosis of the situation. She'd then build enthusiasm and hope with the client team by listing the structures, processes, people, skills, and governance they would need to make impactful improvements. She led client teams to build those unbreakable bonds that only come from going through turbulent times together.

Day in and day out, Felicia delivered on her word in terms of outcomes and timelines for clients, which enhanced their love for her. Her extensive knowledge and experience immediately translated into regained client confidence. Simply put, they knew they were in great hands with her. So, for Felicia, success came from going into the trenches with her clients and helping them find the way out of the situation with clear communication and positive encouragement along the way.

Unfortunately, her Fixer mentality didn't meet her *internal* team's view of success, which is why we began working together.

She had a knack for going into client meetings, letting them know they were going to make tough decisions, giving them options and scenarios, and convincing them they were in it together. Conversely, she wasn't as optimistic or encouraging with her internal team. She had a reputation for being dominating, negative, and critical. She'd express how she couldn't believe they had "messed up," going so far as to say she was *embarrassed* for them. She had a tendency to show her team she didn't trust their judgment by taking work away from them and putting it on her own plate. The two different versions of Felicia—Client Felicia and Boss Felicia—had her team reeling.

When going through the impact statements, the common thread was that the stakeholders agreed she was a powerhouse when it came to client work. But they wanted the Felicia who showed up in front of the clients to be more present with them as an internal team leader. Many of her team members expressed that they didn't want to work with her due to her negative treatment and the way she made them feel untrustworthy.

Beyond this, they were genuinely concerned for her health! Felicia's success over time had been generated from putting out one fire at a time, but as her career progressed in the firm, there were simply too many clients for her to take on each and every one all alone. Without enlisting the help of others, her team could see she wasn't getting enough rest. They wanted to learn how to be great Fixers for clients too, but she just didn't have the energy or insight to delegate projects.

One stakeholder nailed it when they said this:

> *"Felicia can be extremely enjoyable to work with. She can form deep connections and make you feel important and valued... On the other hand, if she judges you or doesn't align with you, she can be dismissive and distracted, even to the point of writing you off. She is probably not conscious of this impact on others, but it does damage to relationships and performance."*

This last sentence in particular shows she really didn't know what impact she was making on her team. She was stuck in the blind spot, telling herself, "I was hired to fix things, so I must dominate others and tell them what to do."

She was so intent on being the Fixer that when the CEO asked her to work with me toward the end of her first year with the company, she was blown away—and definitely *not* in a good way. From her perspective, going through coaching would only give her one more thing to do and have an adverse effect on her effectiveness. She was hired to solve problems, not sit around talking to a coach and getting further behind on her *real* work.

To ease her into the process, I gave her a copy of my book *Work Smart* and asked her to read some of it before deciding whether she wanted to work with me. Thankfully, the content in the first chapter "W for Well" resonated with her, especially as she read about the value of mindset, health, sleep, and nutrition—and she knew those were areas in her life that needed *fixing.* Her husband was also enjoying my book and pointed out how stressed she'd been and all the sleepless nights she'd had. With those two sources nudging her forward, she decided to give coaching a try.

We began with her writing about some of her personal experiences with leaders who had supported her in the past, and I asked her to describe what she admired about them. Once Felicia did this, she could see on paper how the individuals she listed had all put *her* in tough situations and helped guide her through challenges. They had trusted her and given her the space to learn and grow with each new opportunity. Then she compared those experiences to her own behaviours with her internal team. Immediately, she was able to see how her impact wasn't aligned with her intentions at all. When faced with this,

Felicia realized her actions wouldn't get her on her own list of leaders she admired.

As a result, she made a conscious effort to treat her internal team the same way she'd treat clients. She adopted a new, simple rule for herself: if she wouldn't say it to a client, she wasn't going to say it to a team member.

Another breakthrough came when she began to understand she wasn't "fit for human consumption" when she was overworked and grumpy from lack of sleep. This reminded me of a candy bar commercial when I was young, where a person would be featured completely unhinged until their friend hands them the candy bar, as if to say, "Hey—you're not being yourself. Take a bite and reset." In this way, Felicia had to be her own best friend and learn to recognize when she was in a bad mood, then take the time required to reset before interacting with her team.

As she elevated through focusing on both her self-care and others-awareness, Felicia could see her internal team members gain confidence in her leadership. One team member said they were happy to see her smile finally because they couldn't recall seeing her smile even once in the previous year they'd worked together!

By redefining success for herself on a more holistic level, she saw the need for delegation. Felicia trained her internal team to replicate her strengths as a Fixer, using some of the strategies, patience, and nurturing skills she had found to be effective with clients. Before long, there was a team of the *right* kind of Fixers working together to help even more clients get out of tough situations.

It's been a while since I worked with Felicia, but every time we meet up, she hugs me and tells me how that season of coaching changed her life, inside and outside of work—even though she had been reluctant at first. I like to remind her that what made all the difference was her own willingness to accept the feedback with an open mind and consciously make changes.

 ## Devin: The Driver

Devin is a partner in a digital transformation firm that offers cutting-edge solutions to companies whose processes need a more streamlined approach. As a thought leader, he has authored bestselling books in his field, and he has published many articles in major publications. This all makes him a highly sought-after consultant who is recognized and appreciated by many notable experts in the tech industry.

In his role, he works with companies to drive down costs and raise their profits, saving them time and money by implementing the best technological solutions. He's an amazing person with a serious knowledge base, comfortable working with the most experienced people at the highest levels of the organization, and a driving view of success that makes him, well, the "Driver."

For Devin, success meant "making things happen for clients." His passion lies within his ability to share technology as the key differentiator to drive growth and market capitalization, laser-focused on helping companies apply digital transformation technology. His eye for innovating on the manufacturing floor and shifting manual work into automated operations helps clients leap into the future.

Being a Driver led Devin to the conclusion that the most important part of a business is making an impact to the bottom line. He would make bold predictions about how implementing a specific system would save the client $100 million—and then get it done. He would often put his own consultation fees on the line because he knew he would drive the bottom-line results they needed.

As a consultant, his Driver mindset continued to serve him well. He viewed success as creating growth in the firm's bottom line too. And why not? Companies were lining up to work with his firm and paying extremely high fees for him to lead their transformation. His confidence and reputation for delivering what he promised drove clients to him consistently.

When he went to work for a new firm to exponentially grow their digital practice, he hit the ground running just as any Driver would. He was focused on making sales by convincing clients how technology would change their lives for the better. As you might imagine, he was getting noticed for making incredible progress in a short time.

So, why did this Driver want to work with me? After all, he was making the sales, winning awards, and bringing in more happy clients. As his first year at the firm was coming to a close, he was contributing to the bottom line in a massive way—but he was also isolating himself. His peers felt alienated, his leaders were beginning to feel threatened by his seemingly obsessive work ethic, and people were signaling that they didn't want to work for him.

When we began working together, there was a clear consensus in the impact statements. In his stakeholders' points of view, he had crossed the line from confidence to arrogance—and it wasn't a good look for him. Yes, he was highly skilled, but they hoped he could regain some humility and cross the bridge back to professional confidence.

His Driver mentality led him to keep his foot on the gas at all times, making sales and overpromising, which led to some of his team members feeling like he was working them to death. Other times, he'd underestimate the effort required to make good on his promises to the clients, and when team members expressed their concern, they felt like he was quick to write them off.

As they fell behind, he'd either make them feel like he was pounding them into the ground or jumping ahead of them, taking over their part of the work altogether. Some stakeholders felt like he'd make a sale and run, abandoning them, and leaving them to keep a promise they had never made.

Many of the stakeholders expressed feelings of burnout and being undervalued when Devin won awards for projects that had required a ton of work on their part. He'd publicly accept the awards, neglecting to acknowledge the many people whose work had made the award possible. It was all about *him* and his success.

In other words, we had a *lot* to unpack. Devin's view of success was driving him to get the results he felt were the most important, but it was also driving people away from the company. People expressed that they were burned out by him— or specifically did not want to work with him. As a result, the company was facing a high turnover rate. It was time to help this Driver go after the results that would make his firm successful as a *team*. In order to recruit and retain the people with top skills, he needed to have versatility in his approach with people.

We talked about leadership and the importance of seeing people through the lens of what they need in a leader as individuals. Just as people have different views of success, they also have unique perspectives on what makes a great leader.

For instance, some people stated they'd like to work more collaboratively with Devin. Others wanted the chance to get to know each other better as people instead of feeling siloed from the rest of the team. And there were also team members who preferred to complete tasks on their own, knowing they could always come to him if they needed something rather than be micromanaged every step of the way.

There were also signs showing that women didn't want to work for Devin. The company was working hard to have more diversity in the industry, and this trend was putting his reputation at risk. On a personal level, he was an advocate for his two daughters and wanted them to be able to have amazing careers. Learning that women at the firm expressed their negative experiences of working with him hit him hard. This proved to be the eye-opener that helped him see that he needed to make some changes.

Like with Felicia, one of Devin's biggest shifts was also a writing exercise. He wrote the names of the people he felt were critical to his success. I was surprised to see how long the list was! It opened his eyes to the fact that he wasn't creating success all on his own. Once the list was complete, he ranked each person on a scale of one to ten on how much he thought they liked working with him. This sparked a new conversation because we noticed he had many threes and fours. It was time to tap into his others-awareness and create stronger relationships with his internal team.

We drove toward getting those numbers up for the people he depended on the most. He started to have conversations with them by asking questions, including expressing curiosity about their view of success and what results they were driving toward.

We worked on tapping into the natural motivators within people, and he started to incorporate these individual-focused drivers in his people strategy. As a result, the team now saw him as a path to *their* personal success rather than seeing themselves as victims of his success.

Devin started asking, "What would make this a great year for you? How can I support you? What do you need from me?" At first, it was a little unnerving for him to ask those questions to the people on his list, especially when the views they shared were so different from his presumptions. But over time, learning how others view success helped him redefine his own view and create a new definition that better aligned with this state of his career. Connecting to the emotions of their motivations drove him to want to help them achieve their goals.

As a result, he started to be the supportive Driver his team needed him to be rather than the unrelenting Driver he used to default to. Since our time together, Devin has created a core team who meets together to create a joint vision of success. He's actively involved in the recruiting process and contributing to the diversity of his team. And I'm pleased to say that he has found some real champions in the women who work with him now.

Lucas: The Loyalist

A rarity these days, when I met Lucas, he had been with the same company for twenty-five years. When we look at tenure statistics from the US Department of Labor's Chief Evaluation Office in their 2022 report, that is about five times the median tenure held by males![5] Right from our first meeting, I could see the importance Lucas placed on being loyal to his company. Having worked his way up from an entry-level position to a senior vice president position meant he knew a lot about the processes he and his teams were responsible for. He'd gained a reputation for being a leader who knew more about his corporate bank and the entrepreneurs it served than anyone else on the payroll.

In particular, Lucas was known for his quick problem-solving, creativity, and innovation when it came to making deals. He moved up the ranks in so many different regions, management roles, and sectors that he acquired a vast amount of legacy knowledge.

The CEO respected Lucas's instincts and would often pull him aside to get his opinion on various problems. Lucas felt great about having the ear of the CEO, and their relationship grew

---

[5] U.S. Bureau of Labor Statistics, "Employee Tenure Summary," news release, September 22, 2022, https://www.bls.gov/news.release/tenure.nr0.htm#.

based on mutual trust and camaraderie. Creating relationships and helping his boss and team feel heard and supported made Lucas the picture of the "Loyalist."

As a Loyalist, everyone knew Lucas had his heart in the right place. When he was given a mandate, there was no doubt he would follow through and absolutely rock it. There was a feeling of security, knowing the company, his team, and the clients were always in good hands when Lucas was in charge. He viewed success as creating strong relationships and making all of his people feel supported so they could perform at optimal levels and achieve those quantifiable goals.

It's great to have an executive who is willing to stand up for his team, right? Loyalty is a key characteristic for any great leader, but as his role evolved, his notion of the people who deserved his loyalty did not evolve. Lucas struggled to grasp that, as a senior executive, his team was the *entire company*, not just the group of people working directly with him. These limits he placed on his role as a Loyalist created the blind spots which led to coaching.

Lucas had held many different roles within the company, and with each role, he'd build his own silo of success around his boss and the team he was working with. He also tended to build an impenetrable moat around the silo, which kept everyone else at a distance. His internal motto had become "You want me to be accountable for results, so I need to be focused on my scope and solve for *my team*."

In other words, his first priority was always his fierce loyalty to his team of direct reports. In his boss's management meetings with his peers, Lucas would hear a topic and immediately ignore everyone else at the table and begin talking about how to use the topic to solve for his team.

One of the stakeholders pointed this out by stating:

> *"He doesn't demonstrate a senior management mindset where he is focused on the best decision for the bank overall."*

The stakeholder went on to explain how Lucas had worked on teams whose leaders had a similarly siloed mentality for a number of years. The stakeholder suggested that maybe those experiences taught Lucas that this was the only way to drive accountability since he seemed to be following in those leaders' footsteps.

There was a consensus that if Lucas wanted to eventually move into a COO role (the next level up for him), he'd have to demonstrate that he could support the bank as a whole. His peers and the people working above Lucas were frustrated with the way he would argue with them when he didn't agree with the consensus of the management team—usually because he perceived that the decision would negatively impact his direct team. Impact statements indicated he would take a deep dive into arbitrary details with the goal of just wearing his peers down enough until they'd give in to his agenda.

At one point, there was a mandate to consolidate technology resources into a shared team to save time and money. Yet when it came time for Lucas to discuss moving some of his direct reports to his peer's team, he was unwilling to collaborate. While the person in charge of this initiative was able to collaborate well with all of the other teams, Lucas would only tell him there were no changes required to optimize his team. From his perspective, he was exhibiting his loyalty to his team by keeping this "intruder" from interfering. His leaders, on the other hand, expected him to support the leaders that were driving cross-functional initiatives and show that he could function in an increasingly matrixed organizational structure.

At first, Lucas anticipated his feedback would be amazing. He thought he was uniformly loved by his team and peers. When this wasn't the case, he was beside himself. At his core, as a Loyalist, he was a *giver.* He wanted to be that unshakeable, supportive person who people could go to.

As we looked at the impact statements, his first instinct was to argue with me about the details of a specific situation. His knack for creating a reinterpretation of the feedback was a reflection of his view of success. Instead of letting him drive me into his version of the truth, I had to help him slow down and start to build his others-awareness consciously.

We started by redefining his definition of the team. His default view of who made up his team were the people reporting to him and his boss. The end. But given his elevated role in the company now, we needed to broaden his definition to include the entire company and his peers. There were so many moving parts—operational efficiency of the bank, various side projects, the peers' portfolios, and an end-to-end digital experience for the customer—that involved collaboration *across* silos, not just the success of his direct reports. Rather than doubt the ability of his peers to deliver, he had to learn to trust them to do what was best and support them when he was needed.

Next, we looked at the important concept of celebrating collective wins. He needed to embrace the fact that when other teams experience success, it raises the entire company. There didn't need to be an "us against them" mentality. He could be a better Loyalist to everyone by celebrating the wins of his peers.

In order to recreate those relationships that had gone the wrong way for him, Lucas and I practiced his use of one tiny word: *yes*.

In improvisation, actors use a technique known as "Yes, and..." It means that no matter what the other actor says, you have to agree and go with the flow. That is essentially what Lucas started to practice with his peers and team members. When anyone

DIFFERING VIEWS OF SUCCESS

asked him something, he'd say yes—*and* then find a way to align with what they needed. No arguing or disagreeing allowed!

In the end, Lucas began having a lot more fun at work, helping other people by hearing what they wanted and supporting them in their endeavors. His Loyalist nature was able to upgrade to a contributor to everyone's success, and he started to see new loyalty mirrored back to him from his peer group.

The Takeaway

Once the mind has developed its view of success, it almost becomes a heat-seeking missile streaking toward the target. But when those coordinates are a little off, the results can be disastrous.

I had another big shift in my own leadership style when I realized my own view of success needed an upgrade when it came to leading my project status meetings. I used to think that my method was highly efficient as I would launch the meeting and would get "in the zone" with my team. I'd fire out questions— *bang, bang, bang!* My motivation was to get through my questions as quickly as possible, so I knew what needed to be fixed, what *I* needed to escalate, and everything in between. My team meeting was optimized to obtain the information I needed as quickly as possible and get out of there so that everyone could get back to work.

I'd review the status reports before the meeting and proceed to drill people with questions: "Why is this red? Why is this yellow?" and so on. That's how I thought project status meetings should go. But then I heard through the grapevine how much my team *hated* those meetings. Some people couldn't sleep well the night before when they knew their area was struggling. I knew this wasn't right. I needed to make a change so that they didn't dread meeting with me.

My view of success for project meetings changed from getting into the details as quickly as possible to *connecting* with my team instead. Taking a few minutes to check on how everyone was doing and finding small ways to encourage and help each other throughout the meetings made such a difference!

Every leader wants success for themselves and their team. But when our view of success doesn't align with those around us, it can actually derail what we're trying to accomplish and move us *further* away from realizing our goals.

All three of these leaders had views of success that helped them advance in their prospective careers. And because of their own success, they had blind spots making them unaware of how they were creating barriers for others. Their view of success was distracting them from seeing the bigger picture.

Once she faced her blind spots, Felicia was able to mentor others to become Fixers on her team and give them more responsibility, lowering her stress levels. Devin's eyes were opened when he learned how the women on his team felt, enabling him to become a Driver for diversity in his company. By paying attention to and adapting to people's needs, he became determined to create the kind of workplace where his daughters would be happy to work.

Lucas had a view of success that was defined by his core belief that team loyalty created success, but he had failed to upgrade the definition for his team as his role grew and evolved. He had the bandwidth available to make the necessary changes, but he just needed some help clicking the "upgrade" button when it came to his view of success. This rings true for our next blind spot as well, outdated core beliefs.

Often leaders just need to take a step back and look at how things have changed over time since they developed their views on life in general. With some others-awareness and a few tweaks here and there, they can align to an upgraded version of themselves and re-establish their core beliefs to better suit where they are as leaders in real-time.

Summary

How differing views of success happen:	You're focused on a different goal than others.
The shift you need:	Take a step back to recalibrate and align on a target that enables mutual success.
Self-reflection questions to help you uncover differing views of success:	<ul><li>What does success look like to me in my role?</li><li>Who are all the stakeholders that will judge my success?</li><li>What is *their* definition of success for my role?</li><li>What trade-offs do I need to balance so I don't overdo it?</li></ul>

YOUR NOTES

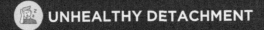

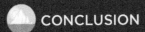

OUTDATED CORE BELIEFS

Simple definition:	Things people do or ways they behave because an underlying belief used to work for them but doesn't anymore.
Root cause:	People's actions are driven by the beliefs they have held for a long time, but these can become destructive when they are outdated.
Often results in:	Victimhood, hypocrisy, burnout

Is it possible to update your beliefs? If so, how do you even begin the process?

Looking back at the previous chapter, each leader had an underlying belief causing misaligned expectations of success within their teams. By taking a step back, we saw how their view of success could evolve to include the voices of their team members. As a result, the leaders and their companies experienced a *new* level of success.

This didn't disqualify their previous successes from earlier parts of their career—it simply evolved their understanding of success. It's a similar situation for our core beliefs.

Core beliefs come in all shapes and sizes, woven together based on the evidence our brains collect, and then translate into our ultimate truth. When our experiences and observations solidify as core beliefs, they show up in both our behaviours *and* our expectations of others. Over time, if we don't give ourselves the space to re-evaluate our core beliefs, we may not be able to see how they're hurting more than helping us.

Many of our core beliefs are imprinted into our subconscious minds without scrutiny when we're young. Our brains *love* patterns and predictability. They're constantly scanning for patterns and proof that form a foundation upon which we build our beliefs.

Often, we don't really understand why we're behaving a certain way. No surprise then when the people around us don't understand it either. They may just notice something is "off" about us, but they don't know why or where it's coming from. And since they can't read our minds, this can develop into frustration on their end.

Have you ever seen the Pixar movie *Inside Out*? The protagonist, Riley, is a twelve-year-old girl who is suddenly moved from rural Minnesota to bustling San Francisco, rocking her world. The main storyline of the film plays out in her head, where we see what the movie calls her "islands of personality," visual depictions of her core beliefs.

One of these is called Family Island. Her family unit has always been strong, so it's formed a central belief for how she identifies herself and her emotional well-being. But the move causes her to feel like she's been betrayed by her parents. Then an argument between her mom and dad only adds to her confusion. Another argument erupts at the family dinner table, prompting her to try to run away back to Minnesota! As a result, Family Island crumbles inside her head.

Her core belief of family unity is shaken by her circumstances because these beliefs were based on her experiences *before* the move. Without giving away too much for those who haven't seen it, she discovers that this core belief in family unity wasn't wrong—but it needed to be updated. It needed to evolve for the family's new context.

Another example can be found in my friend and former client, Tarah, who always knew she wanted to have a family. In many ways, she felt like giving birth to a child was imperative to living a happy life. This was her core belief from as early as she could remember.

But as she wrote about in her book, *Can't Help Falling: The Long Road to Motherhood*, creating a family like the one she grew up in wasn't physically possible for her. This news challenged her core belief, forcing her to face a choice: succumb to the painful belief that her life would be incomplete without biological children or give the belief a little upgrade by planning to adopt. Creating this shift brought with it *new* core beliefs of how she could create a happy life. She chose to move forward *through* the pain by reviewing her beliefs and embracing some upgrades.

Now let's bring this idea into the workplace, where our core beliefs impact not only ourselves but those around us and even the company itself.

We can't control what people believe; however, there are ways to expose when a core belief is outdated, creating unintended conflict. There are ways to discover when it needs to be updated. It's about leading our minds to the proof we need to *reframe* the beliefs that no longer serve us and make room for new beliefs that *do* serve us.

I'll be really frank: the blind spots caused by outdated core beliefs are some of the toughest to expose because beliefs are so tightly connected to our own identities. Even more so than false assumptions or differing views of success, it can feel like a form of self-betrayal to question our own beliefs. Many people aren't willing to do it. But the three examples here prove how leaders can use their stakeholders' feedback as a starting point to dig deep and create the necessary upgrades to bring their leadership to the next level.

 ## Xavier: The Extra-Miler

My client Xavier is a management consultant who advises manufacturing CEOs and boards and is sometimes asked to take on the role of interim CEO for companies undergoing a transition. He is an incredible global leader, born in Asia, raised in Europe, and works with many US-based leadership teams, making his perspectives in international business extremely valuable for many of his clients. His multicultural mindset is a beautiful mix of politeness and loyalty from his birth culture combined with the competitiveness and innovation of the West.

He is absolutely adored by his clients for his intelligence and the way he consistently shows up for them. One impact statement stated Xavier didn't just go the extra mile; he went the "extra 500 miles, all day, every day." He is the poster child of being the "Extra-Miler."

As an Extra-Miler, Xavier seemed to have a superhuman ability to spend exorbitant amounts of time at work with little to no sleep. His kind and helpful demeanor would put clients and team members at ease. His depth of knowledge and high IQ were exhibited without a hint of arrogance. His soft-spoken kindness and extreme generosity with his time were particularly seen as assets within the firm.

Xavier had that rare ability to see things from all angles. He knew the ins and outs of what was happening on the manufacturing floor, in the minds of his clients, and at the top levels of the management all at once. He was proficient at building and maintaining amazing connections through networking. His positive contributions to the business, practice, and people development led another stakeholder to go so far as to gush that Xavier was "99.9 percent perfect."

So, what was the 0.1 percent that motivated his company to invest in coaching for him? Simply put, this man was running himself into the ground. His Extra-Miler persona came from a deeply rooted core belief: "Hard work and going the extra mile to the point of wearing myself out is noble and will be recognized."

While he was certainly being recognized for all his work, the firm also recognized he was either going to literally work himself to death or lose it one day and quit. They didn't want either to happen!

Up to this point, he'd been seen as an incredible leader, but his team members were finding it impossible to live up to the standards Xavier had created for himself. One stakeholder shared the following:

"It was cool to work so many hours and sacrifice your life for work ten years ago, but it just isn't cool anymore."

To clarify, Xavier didn't expect *anyone else* to work all day and then take a red-eye flight to arrive in time for a morning meeting, then sleep for only an hour before hopping on another client call. He never asked others to work late, yet they'd see *him* still at his computer as they left. Another time, he and a team member were both leaving for vacation the next day, but when the client wanted to schedule a nonurgent discussion that conflicted with their vacation, the team member said it would have to wait. What did Xavier do, though? He skipped his vacation to be available for the client. Although he sacrificed himself to handle everything so his team member could enjoy their time off, the team member felt terrible, like they had abandoned Xavier.

Likewise, everyone loved Xavier and appreciated his talent, but they also felt guilty for not sharing his extreme work ethic. If they tried, they found they couldn't match his effort and still have a coherent thought process on so little sleep. Some expressed the sentiment that a sleep-deprived Xavier could *still* run circles around them! It was intimidating, and eventually, people were asking *not* to work with him on projects.

In the impact interviews, it became obvious how more junior people felt intimidated by his extreme work hours, but what was surprising to me was how this was also echoed by his leaders. One senior partner suggested Xavier wasn't acting like a partner because the other partners don't work *all night*. His work intensity and lack of delegation seemed "junior" to them, as they felt he should be leveraging the skills of a team instead. They didn't like when he skipped out on strategic meetings with them to work with clients and felt that his pace and priorities didn't match theirs. They believed that to demonstrate that he was ready to join their ranks, he would need to show that he could set reasonable boundaries for himself and help scale the firm while taking care of his personal health.

Several impact statements also addressed this concern for Xavier's health. They were worried that his body would just shut down one day, and he'd have a heart attack. They knew he was already on blood pressure medication. I was also able to speak with his wife, who also worked in the same industry. While she didn't seem to mind his extra time at work, she really hoped he could make some time to do some things just for *himself,* like playing a sport or taking time off so they could be together. She was especially hopeful he would make more time for their first baby, who was on the way.

Initially, Xavier saw zero issues with doing whatever it took to give the clients an exceptional experience. He never complained about working until 4:00 a.m. or showing up to one of our coaching meetings on only an hour of sleep. While he didn't expect anyone else to send emails at 3:00 a.m., he believed it was necessary for himself.

Revising Xavier's core belief had to go deeper than just discussing how he could set healthy boundaries. We needed to give him some proof that reframing his core belief could give him *new* ways to delight clients.

Xavier's innate compassion for his team members was key to his initial breakthrough. He began by committing to not taking on a job *without* also utilizing the talents within his team. He respected them too much to make them work exorbitant hours, so it helped him to focus on contributing to a few big projects with his team instead of dozens of little projects on his own. We unpacked the outdated belief that he had to be the Extra-Miler and shifted it to the belief that he could create ideal outcomes for all involved while still delivering a delightful customer experience.

He now saw how when he took on projects alone, there was no room for team members to emulate his process and exercise their talents. He agreed only to take on *three* projects at a time, which would allow him more time to develop others and provide more strategic leadership. As a result, Xavier's willingness to spend more time with his colleagues led to him sharing more of his thoughts and ideas, which helped *everyone* on the team to grow.

Think about it this way. As an Extra-Miler by himself, Xavier could only go that extra mile alone. But if ten people on the team could learn from him how to go just an extra 0.2 miles each, not only could they handle this addition to their workload, but the result was a cumulative extra *two* miles.

We also spent some time discussing his paternity leave and his excitement to start a new chapter in his life as a father. He had to gain an understanding of his personal worth *beyond* his output at work. This didn't negate his core belief in being a hard worker—it updated it to gauge his self-worth in a more holistic way.

During the eight-month coaching engagement, Xavier made massive changes in the way he planned his client work and empowered his team. He also achieved his best performance ever in terms of revenue growth and managed delivery. By also taking more time for himself and his family, he now prioritizes his health—especially by sleeping more.

Xavier is also staffing projects by keeping his team members' boundaries in mind. By limiting the number of projects and focusing on engagements with bigger teams, he's generating *more* revenue. Plus, he can now confidently sell larger projects based on realistic expectations. He is becoming more of a leader who models reasonable work-life balance to his team—especially as he steps into a brand-new role as a dad.

Today, Xavier is a proud father and a much more confident leader whose team is benefitting from what he is modeling to them. He learned that the more he can elevate his team, the more miles they can go together. He didn't have to abandon his belief that clients should receive amazing work—but he had to abandon the belief that the work all had to originate from his own hands.

 ## Colin: The Competitor

Core beliefs can be tricky to change when we don't even recognize how they were embedded in our minds during the transition from childhood to adulthood. Sometimes, it takes being triggered by outside influences to get us to be able to see what's really happening on the inside. This was definitely the case with Colin.

Colin's childhood was not easy. He lost his mother at a young age and moved to a different country with his father. Colin watched his father work hard to make ends meet, and they didn't live an extravagant lifestyle by any means. Over time, he formed the core belief that other people may have things easier, but he would have to fight hard to win at the game of life.

He went into finance, driven by his childhood experience of never having enough money. In order to thrive as an adult, he felt a deep urge to understand money and how to make it work for him, which spurred him through college and his MBA. He developed into a transformational expert by working with many different banks, specifically in the realm of enterprise performance from a financial perspective.

Colin is proud of what he was able to achieve in life, largely on his own. He tends to describe his career success as though it was an athletic event, with him playing the part of the self-made "Competitor."

For years, Colin's competitive nature kept him winning with clients. He was engaged and present with them in meetings and had a knack for always asking the right questions. His respect for them made them feel valued and genuinely heard. People could see he wanted to treat them well, which brought him great results. He had gained visible support from senior management, plus a loyal following of people in junior positions who all wanted to work with and learn from him.

As someone who had experienced poverty firsthand, he was (and still is) very empathetic toward those who live in similar situations. He passionately believes everyone deserves to be treated with dignity, no matter their financial circumstances, and tries to model this for his family and community.

Because of this belief, he works hard to remain aware of his humble beginnings and give back to those in need. Before we met, Colin chose to take a year off to travel with his family. He took his wife and their daughters around the world, renting places in impoverished areas. This was primarily motivated by his gratitude for the fruits of his labor. They had an amazing home, and his daughters would never have to worry about money the way he had. Since he had avoided becoming a victim of intergenerational poverty, he wanted his family to see what life was like when people *didn't* have the wealth his hard work had afforded them.

When he came back to work after his year of travel, Colin was given a different job. His old position had been given to a co-worker who we'll call Amanda. Although he wasn't demoted, he felt slighted by the lateral move, like he was somehow losing a job where he had been the reigning champ. As a Competitor, Colin compared himself to Amanda, sizing her up to see if he could win the chance to take on *both* roles.

What he was missing, though, was how the President of his division had strategically placed them in these roles hoping Colin and Amanda would work together as a team. Each role took into account their strengths, and he believed they could be an unstoppable powerhouse. Colin's new role was working directly with the clients, while Amanda was responsible for building out the core offerings and processes. Still, Colin believed in his core that he was getting batted down. He felt like a victim.

As you can imagine, this created conflict, and his leadership wasn't seeing the results they had hoped for. Colin's stakeholders mentioned a distinct difference between the way he worked with clients versus his internal team. Physically, he's a tall and muscular man with a big, booming voice, so it didn't take much for him to come across as intimidating to his coworkers.

Colin also didn't seem to recognize how going on his year-long sabbatical had forced leadership to make changes in the organizational structure. The leadership team had gone out of their way to accommodate his absence and didn't feel Colin appreciated their efforts to support him. As a Competitor, he seemed to feel like he had "won" the sabbatical on his own efforts and that his job was stolen from him.

He was bitter in his new role, and it showed. He became known for his aggressive attitude in meetings, calling out other co-workers on their perceived flaws. While his intention may have been to share his knowledge and expertise, it left them feeling put down. Colin was extremely intelligent and articulate, but the Competitor role he took on kept him in a mindset of constantly having to prove himself to those around him. It made his team uncomfortable, believing all he wanted to do was fight them.

Colin was also putting pressure on his leaders for a promotion. Still, the feedback from many of the impact statements revealed that his leaders felt he was demonstrating a lack of maturity since he returned from his leave. When he was met with this information, his immediate response was to feel victimized, like they weren't being fair with their accusations of immaturity.

The initial feedback felt like a punch to the throat. Then as his rage subsided, he didn't know where to start. He felt hurt. He felt like a victim again. He felt like protesting and escalating the issue since he saw it all as unfair criticism. But I urged him to refrain from this because it would simply reinforce their perception that he wasn't mature enough to learn from the feedback!

Since we were dealing with core beliefs, we needed to find a way to reset his Competitor nature, specifically the outdated belief that others were receiving preferential treatment and that he had to fight for his rights. Revisiting his feedback, he found a "gem" of an insight: the common thread was that his stakeholders were just asking him to treat his internal team the *same way* he treated his clients. He suddenly realized this was true—his treatment of his internal colleagues was the polar opposite of how he treated clients. He saw he wasn't offering his colleagues—and Amanda in particular—the same respect, dignity, and openness he afforded his clients.

Over time, his competitive spirit had given him an unhealthy detachment from their feelings, so he tapped into his others-awareness. As a leader with a huge humanitarian heart, Colin felt conflicted about letting his emotions get the best of him. He was always stressing to his family the importance of treating everyone with equal value, yet he had been hypocritical when he got caught up in victim mode at work.

This "Eureka" moment was just the shift Colin needed. He redefined his core belief by deciding his job was to embody the care, gratitude, and respect that every human being deserves. He needed to model the compassion he and his father had failed to receive when he was young. He then worked to integrate this new core belief in every facet of his life, including his work. Colin learned how fun it was to collaborate with Amanda as a fellow human being, and I'm proud to say they just keep winning together!

Since then, Colin has been using his compassion for others by leading initiatives within the firm to help serve families in underprivileged communities. During his debrief with his boss following our program together, his boss literally cried, telling Colin he always knew he had such an amazing heart for others but just needed to see it deployed internally. Now that Colin is choosing to compete as a team player, there are no limits to the collateral benefits possible from his updated core beliefs.

Erica: The Expert

Before joining the workforce as a senior leader in IT, Erica spent over twenty years in the military working as a tech specialist in systems engineering. She had lived in a world where creative risk-taking and experimentation didn't cut it. Instead, you followed the standard operating procedures, or people could be in *serious* danger. Her decades of knowledge and the way she could tackle the most difficult client projects with amazing project management skills created a person with machine-like efficiency, which is why I like to call her the "Expert."

As an Expert, Erica was extremely client-centric—and clients loved her. When she walked into a room, she was the epitome of confidence, immediately evoking a sense of safety and security for them, no matter what issues the client was facing. Many of the impact statements praised her communication style, describing her as respectful, formal, and poised.

Senior members of the company also felt that Erica was extremely professional when they interacted with her. If she didn't understand something, she knew how to ask the right questions to gain the clarity necessary to give informed status updates to her clients. They appreciated the systems she implemented to make things more streamlined and saw how she went above and beyond expectations in the project management component of her role.

But the junior members of the company saw a completely different version of this Expert. When formal complaints started rolling in, the senior members didn't want to lose Erica, so they asked me if I could help. Specifically, they wanted me to support her in sorting out what was happening to earn all this negative attention from her internal team.

What I discovered in my interviews was how Erica the Expert was a very *rigid* leader. Given her long history and high rank in the military, she seemed to have developed a core belief that there can only be one right way of doing things. And more often than not, the right way was *her* way. In the military culture she was used to, when something was mission-critical, they had to follow orders, or people could literally die. While this thinking had served her well in the military, when Erica implemented these militaristic tactics in a company made up of young civilians, it backfired. The higher the intensity of the project, the more triggered she'd become. And the more she felt a deeper level of stress, the more she presented like a drill sergeant to her "inferiors," that is, the junior members of the company.

If a mistake was made, she'd let them know in no uncertain terms that they were bad at their job. Her way of trying to course-correct felt demeaning, almost to the level of emotional abuse. Junior members began going above her head, forwarding her hurtful emails to the senior members. These leaders were shocked—the reported behaviours were so at odds with the Erica they had interacted with.

Predictably, Erica's response to stress was always *fight.* One stakeholder suggested Erica should take a moment when she feels emotional before exploding in a meeting or firing off an aggressive email. Another stakeholder recalled a day when she received one such blistering email—yet Erica had misunderstood the context of the problem. This could have been avoided if she had simply asked for some clarity first.

Yet another team member explained how this Expert could improve her interactions with junior members:

"Erica is able to soften and adjust her messages because she does this beautifully when she engages in discussions with her leaders. She respects their authority, and she communicates with authenticity and a high degree of professionalism."

Yet they wanted to see this behaviour modeled with *everyone*, not just the people she viewed as her superiors in the "chain of command."

This incredible feedback showed Erica proof that she was absolutely capable of maintaining a professional tone even under stress. She already possessed the skills to create trust and maintain good relationships with her team members. She just needed to use them consistently.

The impact statements also helped to provide some insight for Erica into how she was still relating to others from a hierarchy mindset. She was working hard to impress those above her while simultaneously looking down on those who were beneath her "rank," expecting them to obey her without question.

These core beliefs had served her well for two and a half decades spent in a different culture with a different set of standards and rules to live by. Now they were outdated and needed to be revised and updated.

First, we had to uncover the trigger point for her. What was the unstoppable intention driving her behaviour? In our conversations, it became obvious that the stress of doing a good job caused her to become critical of others in an intense and reactive way. This led us to focus on the way Erica managed stress. She needed to master the tools of settling down before reacting. She interrupted this behavioural pattern by learning to appreciate others, seeing their positive intentions, and reframing how she judged their competence.

Next, we looked at her outdated core belief that every "mission" in the company was a military operation. Yes, projects felt intense at times, but there was never the imminent danger of "life or death." Working with juniors who were primarily millennials, she had perceived their need for creativity and flexibility as insubordination. She had to learn how giving them some freedom to create their own solutions would help them learn and grow—instead of telling them they were incompetent because they weren't following *her* specific protocol.

We discussed how she had so much wisdom to offer the juniors, and frankly, in a hot market like theirs, they could exert free will and choose *not* to work with her. She needed a way to earn their followership rather than simply expect it, demand it, or bully them into it.

In one session, we discussed her practice of referring to the new graduates as "documenters" instead of by their names. Their actual title was Technical Analyst, an entry-level position responsible for testing and creating documentation for the system. No one minded the testing component of the role, but documentation was hands down their *least* favourite part of the job. When Erica called them "documenters," she belittled them by referring to their least favourite part of the job.

At first, Erica didn't understand why this was such a big deal to them, especially given that documentation *was* a part of their job. So, I offered her an example to see if she could understand how it could be problematic:

"I'm sure there are some people in the world who love to do laundry," I explained, "but I am *not* one of those people! So, if my son came home from school, saw me doing laundry, and called me 'Laundry Lady' instead of Mom, I'd lose it!"

This helped her understand why she should call them by their *names* or *titles* as a sign of respect. She had to see everyone as *equals* who were all working toward the same goal, regardless of their "rank." If she could treat clients and executives well, she could do the same with the juniors.

Also, we discovered that Erica's mind was quite fixated on finding people's weaknesses. Instead, I asked her to experiment with becoming strengths-focused, to continually look for the skills each individual brought to the table. She needed to stop looking at everything people *couldn't* do and focus on what they *could* do. Then she could evolve into a powerful influence by encouraging them to implement those strengths into their jobs.

We also worked to move away from her core belief that she was the only one who knew what was best for the company. In time, she updated to the new belief that her job was to maximize the collective intelligence of her team. This shift allowed Erica to create a positive environment for everyone to develop as individuals who were simultaneously contributing to the best interests of the company and their clients.

When core beliefs have been crucial to our past success, it takes concerted, conscious effort to make the changes to align them to a new environment. Sometimes stress would show up and Erica would instinctively slip back into the core belief that the mission had to be accomplished at all costs, no matter the collateral damage caused in her wake.

Instead of jumping into "fight" mode, Erica had to learn to step back and gauge her emotions. When they were running high, she learned to take some time to breathe and calm herself before rushing in and tearing people apart. When she was frustrated, she started writing down *why*. Then she could reassess the situation, exercising the new core beliefs she was cultivating.

Erica came up with some prompts she could ask herself about different team members to help her see them in a more positive light. For example, she would ask herself, "What is their true talent, and how can it be used here? Is it possible their approach will lead to the same outcome?" These questions helped her shift away from the automatic assumption that her juniors were just incompetent or insubordinate.

We also created a rule: "People need to feel better at the end of every meeting with you." If they came in feeling neutral or anxious, it was her new mission to make sure they left feeling excited about all of the good work everyone was creating as a team. With these updated core beliefs, Erica continues to take the necessary steps to gain the trust, respect, and followership of her team members.

In fact, junior people are now *asking* to work with her because they are learning so much. They are no longer intimidated or offended by her behaviour, which is a *huge* win. Erica's leaders are thrilled with the transformation and the "expert" contribution she is making to accomplish the company's mission of serving their clients.

The Takeaway

Core beliefs are so rooted in our subconscious that they can feel like unchangeable personality traits or instinctual behaviours. When we see success after success by following these beliefs, it becomes even more difficult to see a need for change.

In the movie *Inside Out*, part of why Riley decides to run away is because of her core belief that her role in the family is always to be happy and positive. When her sadness about the move creeps in, it shatters this belief, and she loses the sense of who she is at her core. By the end of the film, she realizes she doesn't always have to be the happy kid—she can show her true feelings to her parents. When she does, her core beliefs get an update, and Family Island is rebuilt stronger than ever.

Xavier's belief in hard work is so common for leaders and played a key role in his success, so no wonder he didn't initially see how it was becoming a roadblock to his success. Colin's competitive nature had helped him win at work and set up generational wealth, but he had to learn how to compete as a team, not just as an individual. Erica's military mindset had helped her protect people and earn higher ranks, but she had to let go of seeing everything as "mission critical" in the corporate world.

Although their core beliefs brought them success in one phase of their journey, those beliefs became outdated, like old software, creating a gap between their intentions and impact. Yet all these leaders were able to then obtain an even greater level of success through their willingness to make the shift and update those beliefs.

Changing beliefs requires reflection and repetition of new beliefs. Automated repetitive thoughts in our minds solidify outdated core beliefs. To make new core beliefs, we need to bombard our minds with new repetitive thoughts. To aid in this process, I often make recordings of affirmations to reinforce the new beliefs. Many of my clients listen to these once per day for months so they can take root and grow. Upgrading your core beliefs is one of the greatest investments you can make.

If you would like to try forming some new healthy core beliefs, you can **download this free daily affirmation meditation** at www.leaderley.com/dailyaffirmation

Listen to it for fourteen days before deciding if you want to continue. You may find upgrading your core beliefs feels pretty good.

Erica's core beliefs were driving many unconscious habits that had to be corrected over time. When we can use our self-awareness to identify outdated core beliefs, it's easier to bring these unconscious habits into the light. Once we can fully recognize these habits and actions and how they affect those around us, it becomes easier to make the necessary changes and uplevel our performance. Ready to tackle your unconscious habits?

Summary

How outdated core beliefs happen:	You have a belief that was true at one point but now it needs to evolve.
The shift you need:	Upgrade your beliefs by replacing them with more relevant or empowering ones.
Self-reflection questions to help you uncover outdated core beliefs:	• How do my beliefs need to adapt to my current situation? • What attributes have I developed that I believe are critical to my success? • Which of these may be outdated or are creating conflict? • Where do I need to give myself permission to change?

YOUR NOTES

....

....

....

....

....

....

....

....

....

....

....

....

....

....

....

....

 INTRODUCTION

BLIND SPOTS

FALSE ASSUMPTIONS

UNHEALTHY DETACHMENT

DIFFERING VIEWS OF SUCCESS

OUTDATED CORE BELIEFS

 UNCONSCIOUS HABITS

TRIGGERS FROM PAST PAIN

MISMATCHED MINDSETS

UNCOVERING BLIND SPOTS

CONCLUSION

UNCONSCIOUS HABITS

Simple definition:	Things people do or ways they behave that inadvertently annoy others or hold them back.
Root cause:	People's habits are symptoms of underlying thought patterns that were once conscious and helpful but have become unconscious and unhelpful over time.
Often results in:	Resistance, overwhelm, impatience

When we think of habits, we could probably classify many of them as the actions we take without involving much brain power. Consider your own daily routine. You might shower in the morning, brush your teeth, grab some coffee, and drive to work, seemingly all on autopilot. And although your body has built up the corresponding muscle memories over time, you still have to consciously *choose* to do each of these routines.

For instance, if you run into heavy traffic one morning and you're running late, you may decide to skip the coffee run. And although starting the day without coffee can be annoying, it's a choice. You have the free will to alter your actions, including your habits.

Unconscious habits are the actions we take that are so deeply integrated into who we *think* we are, we have no active awareness of them. We chalk them up as just part of our personalities and settle in for a lifetime of not only accepting these unconscious actions but even justifying them as unchangeable.

While some unconscious habits (like brushing your teeth) can be good, blind spots arise when the actions and reactions we repeat fuse with our identity. When others only see us as a habit and not as a person, it can cause collateral damage all around us.

I like to compare the unconscious-habits blind spot to running an algorithm within your brain. We all have thousands of these algorithms running simultaneously, and each one has a point of origin, moving from one neuron to another. We can stop running an algorithm or start running a different one, but we first must bring consciousness to the established algorithm running on autopilot. We have to decide to disrupt it before we can replace it.

Otherwise, any of us can easily fall into the thought pattern of *Well, this is just who I am. There is nothing I can do about it, so deal with it.* But it doesn't take a mountain of wisdom to see how damaging this mentality can be.

Creating new thought patterns is hard, though. It means we first have to take a step back and become curious about *why* we behave the way we do. Once we can identify the patterns that need to change, we can take responsibility for them and make conscious changes that will become more automatic the more we use them. The good news is that there are ways to consciously change your behaviours while also changing your thought patterns. When your behaviours and thoughts become aligned to new patterns, you develop a new habit.

Our three leaders here were so unaware of their unconscious habits that they couldn't see how they had actually become their own worst enemies. We'll discover three different patterns of self-sabotage that led them to damage not only their team members but their own credibility. The fun part about this particular blind spot, though, is how each leader was able to get curious, take responsibility, and ultimately make new choices that enhanced their leadership skills in ways they couldn't have imagined!

 ## Adam: The Achiever

When he was a young child, Adam immigrated with his family to North America. Despite their highly educated backgrounds, his parents struggled to find work, so they opened a dry-cleaning business. Adam grew up among the racks of clothing, working in the family business when he wasn't in school—and he hated every minute of it.

He was frustrated his parents had chosen dry cleaning to build a livelihood when they'd had more "esteemed" jobs before. He felt out of place in his new home, where he noticed how different his family was from everyone else. There weren't any other brown faces to be found, and his family were the only members of their religious minority in their small town. When Adam realized later that he was gay, the sense of isolation only deepened as he found himself a minority within a minority. At the same time, the frustration he felt about the big and little things day after day, year after year, also fueled him to prove himself—and prove himself he did by becoming the "Achiever."

As an Achiever, Adam continuously strove for the next level. He decided he'd get a law degree rather than continue with the family's dry-cleaning business, which he not-so-secretly despised. Not only did he reach his goal, but he took advantage of his great intellect and thrived in his career. The never-satisfied attitude of this Achiever brought a great reputation for his abilities to handle the complexities of long-term contract law, and he soon became one of the most sought-after corporate lawyers in North America.

Adam was known to come into a new case and hit the ground running. He'd look through the contract and find the areas that required stronger wording, places where the team may have missed some important points, and then deliver suggestions on how to improve the contracts. The Achiever in him could *always* find the flaw, and he always seemed to know the exact next best step.

When I met Adam, the partners at the firm wanted to promote him to top leadership. They loved his attention to detail, the way his mind worked, and how wildly successful he was. They felt grateful to have him on the team, and a promotion would go a long way in ensuring they could retain his irreplaceable talent. But they had one concern: Adam had a reputation for alienating himself from the other lawyers he was supposed to collaborate with.

The partners had received so much negative feedback from Adam's peers and team members that they simply couldn't say he was a shining example of what they valued in a leader. While his work on paper was impeccable, his interpersonal relationships were the exact opposite. Even with the firm's clients, some reported they appreciated his honesty, but many of them were offended by the way he chose to deliver it.

One day, Adam was confronted with this reality when he found out he would not be included in the company newsletter diversity spotlight. Even though he was a prominent example of diversity among the leadership team, his profile was declined specifically because of his reputation for being difficult to collaborate with.

The partners felt his Achiever mentality, which had brought him so much individual success, was now preventing him from being a team player. How could they position him to lead the organization when he had proved he preferred to act as "a lone wolf" prowling on the fringe of the pack?

While going through the impact statements, it was clear Adam had different standards for his behaviour compared to how he related to others. For example, Adam didn't tolerate tardiness from other lawyers, yet he sent very mixed messages when he himself would show up late—or even call in to important meetings while running errands, jumping in and out disruptively. He had a habit of walking into a meeting late and finding a flaw that would compel the team to start all over. Had he been on time, though, they could have addressed the flaw sooner and saved everyone's time and energy.

Also, he would complain about not having enough time in a day to help others but would expect everyone to drop everything to address part of a contract that had previously been approved and closed. This caused rework and *more* time for the team rather than moving forward from an agreed-upon starting point. So much habitual hypocrisy left other lawyers feeling anxious and on edge when they knew Adam was on their team for a new project.

Adam also *underinvested* in developing relationships, which was interpreted as a lack of concern for others. The consensus was that Adam simply didn't care to get to know anyone on his peer or junior teams. He presented as emotionally disconnected from them entirely. And with his nose-to-the-grindstone attitude, they didn't get a chance to know much about who he was as a person. They knew him only as a whirlwind of frustrated energy and insults who swirled around their offices, never knowing when he'd show up and add an extra splash of chaos to their day.

His gut reaction to their honest feedback was indignance and—you guessed it—frustration. His inner (and outer) dialogue was something like, "*How dare they throw me under the bus when they know full well I'm the one who came in and saved the day? I'm the smartest one in the room and continuously fixing their messes!*"

For Adam, a big first step was helping him slow down and strengthen his self-awareness in order to get him into a space where he could handle others-awareness. We began by looking at the fundamentals of good leadership, specifically with his connections (or lack thereof) with the junior and peer lawyers. Many of the stakeholders were simply asking for him to be on time and present at meetings. We discussed the difference between what he expected from others and how they experienced the opposite from him. He came to realize he presented a "do as I say and not as I do" mentality.

Additionally, we searched for ways he could still address the flaws he saw in contracts while also showing appreciation for all of the work the team had put in. He needed to put effort into understanding who people were and listen to where they were coming from rather than just show up and expect them to get on board "the Adam Train" without any explanation.

His "Eureka" moment came when he realized our coaching was due to the desire of leadership to eventually promote him. Up until then, he had assumed they were just gathering evidence to fire him. Instead, he was surprised to learn they *wanted* to move him to the next level, which was the only reason they had endured all his frustrated outbursts, imperfections, and negative feedback. But now he had to first help himself by making the changes they needed in a next-level leadership role.

Some spectacular shifts began when he saw how his false assumptions and suspicions were totally wrong.

Adam's biggest unconscious habit was that his default response was set to "frustration." For example, he perpetually reacted negatively to every email he opened, interpreting each one as an attack. So, we decided to start there. Rather than assume the email was an assault, he had to read all work emails as though they were love letters. This silly game gave him the opportunity to *consciously* interact with a completely different tone than what his habit had been.

I shared my triple-A formula from my TEDx talk and he applied it to formulate his email responses. The first sentence had to contain a statement of appreciation. He'd follow this with a statement that aligned with the other person's perspective and then finish with one—*and only one*—augment, i.e., a suggestion for improvement. The template was:

> I appreciate...
>
> I align with...
>
> I would consider... (to *augment* rather than *diminish*)

When going over documents, he worked on being more curious. It was no longer acceptable to tap into a flurry of frustration and highlight a myriad of flaws without knowing the proper context. Instead, he started asking the writer about their thoughts behind specific sections of a contract. This opened the door to *coaching* instead of *reacting.* Team members now felt heard, and Adam had the chance to share his thoughts and help them learn from him instead of just directing them. This new approach opened dialogue, creating professional depth and empowering team members to grow their own skills.

Also, Adam now saw the hypocrisy in striving for excellence and craving recognition and appreciation from others even though he was withholding any recognition or appreciation from them. By realigning his intentions to match the desired impact for his team, Adam let go of frustration and embraced gratitude. He moved from an attitude of *How dare you?* to a genuine attitude of *Thank you!*

Seeing his unconscious habits and making the conscious decision to change them helped Adam grow closer to his team. He learned to actively stop taking things so seriously and share his sense of humor with the other lawyers. Also, he implemented "storytime" by dedicating a few moments at the beginning of his meetings for people to get to know each other better as human beings. This allowed him to share the story about his own upbringing and how those difficulties had shaped his life. As other team members shared their stories, their camaraderie grew too.

Since our coaching together, I've been able to check in with Adam and his stakeholders, who consistently report the one-eighty he's made. The Adam they now see was always there, hidden underneath the unconscious habits. He had to make the choice to peel those layers back so they could see the *real* Adam. With this new understanding of himself and others, I can't wait to see how much more he is able to achieve.

 ## Gretchen: The Giver

Companies could spend a lifetime looking for a leader like Gretchen and never find anyone close to her. She had developed an amazing followership because people knew she was always there to support them in finding growth opportunities. She was the epitome of what a company wants in a mentor: nurturing, thoughtful, and unafraid to go out of her comfort zone for the good of the team and their clients. Her willingness to consistently go out of her way to help others feel seen, heard, and appreciated is exactly why she is the "Giver."

Clients raved about Gretchen's commitment to their needs. Learning about her Giver mindset, I had a long list of complimentary feedback to go through on the impact statements. People loved her maturity, responsiveness, and organizational skills, just to name a few. Her ability to build relationships seemed to come naturally as she'd take a moment in each meeting to connect with people on a personal level.

In addition to building those authentic relationships, Gretchen was a top-notch consultant. Her assertiveness in the market, mixed with her strong financial background, helped her to listen to her clients, analyze their metrics, and find the best possible solutions.

As a Giver, Gretchen never shied away from the next opportunity. Her sense of accountability and care for others led her to raise her hand to volunteer for the most difficult accounts and the toughest targets. She sounds like a corporate dream come true, right?

But her unconscious habit of taking care of everything and everyone else was backfiring. This Giver reminds me of Shel Silverstein's children's book *The Giving Tree*. Every time the little boy in the story needs something, the tree happily gives it to him until it's nothing but a stump in the end. Luckily for Gretchen, her story has a much happier ending.

My first contact with the company was through Gretchen's colleague and friend. He started by letting me know she was an absolute rock star, but she was coming off a difficult year with her portfolio. People closest to her saw a shift—her light and bubbly personality felt more forced. They could feel her energy diminishing daily. She seemed tired and noted how she just had a "heaviness" about her. She was so supportive of everyone else, but they weren't sure how they could show her the same support when she self-isolated.

Gretchen was so good at giving that she simply didn't comprehend it's okay to be on the receiving end sometimes — especially when you're overwhelmed. To paraphrase her colleague, Gretchen's job is like a marathon, but she was trying to sprint through several marathons at once. Meanwhile, the people who cared about her were becoming increasingly concerned for her health and well-being.

Rather than pressuring her to go through coaching, Gretchen's boss asked her to meet with me for one thirty-minute meeting. In typical Giver style, Gretchen was gracious and initially approached coaching as yet another opportunity for her to grow and stretch beyond her comfort zone. Essentially, she saw it as another way to become more giving.

Still, she was open-minded and honest as we started going over the impact statements. It was like she was a dehydrated sponge just soaking up all this new information. Her Giver nature made her receptive to working with me, but she realized quickly she had to allow herself to be on the receiving end of support and encouragement. Gretchen had to embrace a new idea for her—being a *receiver* could help her better serve her team and clients.

To accomplish this, she had to consciously consider when enough was enough. She had to fight her habit of always saying yes to everybody. Gretchen needed to see that others would be fine if she chose to decline a project. She had team members who knew their own capacity for taking on work, and it was time for her to do the same.

To bring this unconscious habit into her consciousness and change her thought patterns, we first discussed the concept of joy and how it fits into the projects she was working on. When given an opportunity, Gretchen needed to consider how she could approach it joyfully with questions like *If I can't joyfully raise my hand for this, why am I raising my hand at all? If I can't joyfully execute this task, who might be able to help me make it more joyful? Do I just need to delegate it or sit this one out and rest?*

With joy as her measuring line, we altered her internal evaluation criteria when opportunities arose. Rather than looking at the project and assuming it *needed* to be done, I had Gretchen pause and consider whether she thought it would be a fun project for her to take on. If it didn't immediately present itself as fun but still held interest for her, then how could she create some fun?

When she's in a good place energetically, Gretchen lights up a room. The reverse is also true, though. When she's feeling overwhelmed, missed opportunities abound. Taking care of herself and ensuring she has enough adventures outside of work helps her to positively influence others.

One example of creating fun within a project was an international trip she took with some clients. I encouraged her to add a day of sightseeing to her itinerary instead of coming straight home to meet with the next group of clients. Finding ways to orchestrate collateral benefits that would bring Gretchen some personal delight was a way she could "receive" and refill after giving so much to the project.

As a result, a new discipline Gretchen incorporated was to *give* herself a quarterly vacation. Sometimes she would take a week, sometimes just a long weekend, but she would always be planning or looking forward to these self-care breaks. Whenever she returns from one, she immediately books the next one, so she won't miss out on the time she needs to unplug, relax, and revive her spirit.

Gretchen was able to replace her subconscious habit of saying yes to everything no matter how busy she was with a conscious habit of listening to her own needs. She learned to give herself the same level of nurturing that she had previously reserved only for others. Finding a balance between the two has helped her continue to bust through ceilings—without wearing herself out along the way.

And guess what! It worked. By focusing more on joy, she managed to have her best year ever, which earned her an important promotion.

 ## Tessa: The Teacher

When we first met, Tessa was the director of accounting and the only woman on the leadership team in a male-dominated industry. She had a knack for always seeing the positive in every situation. Working in a manufacturing company located in a rural area, she helped raise the brand through philanthropy and community-building, creating goodwill and buzz that the company was an employer of choice.

Beyond this, she was always driving continuous improvement initiatives, which saved the company significant money. Her financial acumen, combined with her savviness for metrics, helped guide their judgment time and time again, which is why Tessa is the "Teacher."

As a Teacher, Tessa brought her expertise and great energy to the projects and initiatives, along with her passion for sharing any business insights provided through the realm of finance. She created positive morale and gained the appreciation and respect of everyone, from the boardroom to the warehouse floor, as "the numbers person."

The CEO asked me to work with Tessa because he wanted to seek the board's approval to promote her to an officer of the company, but first he wanted her to work on some areas where she could refine her leadership. While this Teacher was very knowledgeable in her scope of responsibilities, she also had the unconscious belief that she needed to have *all* the answers to *every* question, which was irritating her peers.

In our coaching sessions, we discovered that the roots of her unconscious habits started in her childhood. She had grown up on a family farm, and while the men in the family did all of the manual labor, Tessa learned early that she loved bookkeeping. She had fond memories of being trusted to count the money they earned at the local farmers' market. This built her confidence as a young girl, seeing how she was gifted with numbers and could contribute to the family. But deep down, she always felt like she had to *prove* her intelligence to those around her.

As the first person in her family to go to university, Tessa had a drive that couldn't be matched. Her perseverance and determination to break the mould eventually made her the breadwinner in her family. She found herself working at a higher-level position than she'd ever imagined, with a salary sufficient to support her stay-at-home husband and children.

She had earned pride and praise along the way for her ability to teach concepts to others, so she continued to leverage her Teacher mentality to go even further in the company.

In fact, her first major assignment was to confidentially investigate the mishandling of the finances by one of the two owners. This "secret mission" further validated her sense of empowerment as she was able to uncover the truth and explain what was happening to other leaders in the company. She had plenty of teaching to do first because she was elevating the maturity of their accounting system and adding finance controls they needed to understand.

In reading her stakeholder interview summaries, Tessa's habits reminded me of the student who sits at the front of the classroom and puts her hand up before the teacher has even finished asking the question. She had an exuberance about her that felt like overenthusiastic engagement to her peers. Her unconscious desire to show up as an expert blinded her to the gap she was creating between her intention and impact.

The impact statements from stakeholders all praised her knowledge in the finance department, but to paraphrase one stakeholder, although she was smart, she needed to continue learning about the industry. Another peer pointed out how in board meetings, Tessa liked to share her opinions about topics outside her area of expertise, which typically led to misinformation and confusion. If the person speaking made eye contact with her, she interpreted it as a cue for a response and would then interject her "knowledge" on the topic—even when this meant the knowledge was wrong or straight-up fabricated.

Tessa's urge to have all the answers put her on a self-sabotaging path. Rather than proving herself to her peers by sharing her perspectives, she was actually single-handedly destroying her credibility within the company.

She was also notorious for having facial expressions that said a lot more than she wanted to share with others. Even when she didn't speak a word, her peers could be put off by her nonverbal cues, another habit she was completely unaware of.

Tessa's intention was good—she wanted to add value. But she needed to find a way to add value without undermining others. What first helped Tessa shift away from being the all-knowing Teacher was to consciously recognize how each person in a room has unique expertise and experience to offer.

For example, rather than going into board meetings poised to speak on anything and everything, she simply began asking her peers where they wanted her input. This gave her a chance to align with them and take note of when she just needed to listen, period. Whether someone made eye contact with her or not, Tessa would stick to sharing her expertise on her agreed-upon line items. This also helped her become more conscious of her nonverbal cues and be more intentional about controlling her facial expressions during meetings.

Another helpful exercise for her was touring the facilities with various people. I then had her come back to me and explain what made each person fascinating and what she had learned from them about their function. As the amazing student she'd always been, Tessa soaked everything in like a sponge. Not only was she learning about the industry from veterans who knew their part of the business inside and out, but she was also earning their respect by being genuinely interested in learning from them. By allowing them to teach her, it made them more open for the opportunities when she needed to teach them.

By making these simple changes, I'm pleased to say Tessa was able to receive a promotion to become CFO and an officer of the company. It was great to see this Teacher learn how there is room in the spotlight for *everyone* and that the best Teachers are always learning and willing to correct their own knowledge along the way.

The Takeaway

One interesting aspect of unconscious habits is how they are much easier for those around us to see. This makes them very different from some of the other blind spots we've addressed thus far that may be hiding from both parties involved. What is glaring to those around us goes completely unnoticed by ourselves, like a sesame seed stuck in our teeth. When we decide to be open to feedback and use it as a mirror, we can then consciously take the steps necessary to replace destructive habits with positive ones.

The biggest thing holding back all of our leaders here was *themselves*. Awareness was the first step to tapping into their unconscious habits. Understanding they could make the choice to form new habits helped each of them to embrace personal growth and make lasting changes.

Adam replaced unconscious frustration with conscious gratitude when he got to know his team at a deeper level. Gretchen learned how being her own version of a "giving tree" had to include taking the time for some personal regrowth. And Tessa learned she could contribute to her team, even when it meant saying nothing and allowing other team members to share their professional insight.

As you may have noticed, many of these unconscious habits not only stemmed from core beliefs that had developed and solidified in their subconscious minds, but these beliefs were also shaped by past pain. Adam's past pain of growing up as a minority had triggered his feelings of professional unfairness, and he would immediately suspect others of trying to undermine his success. When past pains are triggered, they easily lead to beliefs and behaviours that can hold leaders back from finding the success they crave in both work and life.

Summary

How unconscious habits happen:	There is a discrepancy between the actions you take and the actions you need to take.
The shift you need:	Realize and change a destructive-habit pattern by replacing it with a new habit.
Self-reflection questions to help you uncover unconscious habits:	• What regular actions do I take that might negatively impact others? • Which of my regular behaviours are negatively impacting my mood or productivity? • What activities am I *not* doing that could positively impact my mood or productivity? • Which of my regular behaviours most negatively impact others? • What self-care habits am I practicing—or not practicing?

YOUR NOTES

....
....
....
....
....
....
....
....
....
....
....
....
....
....
....

 INTRODUCTION

BLIND SPOTS

FALSE ASSUMPTIONS

UNHEALTHY DETACHMENT

DIFFERING VIEWS OF SUCCESS

OUTDATED CORE BELIEFS

UNCONSCIOUS HABITS

TRIGGERS FROM PAST PAIN

MISMATCHED MINDSETS

UNCOVERING BLIND SPOTS

CONCLUSION

TRIGGERS FROM PAST PAIN

Simple definition:	Things people do or ways they behave to protect themselves.
Root cause:	Painful or traumatic experiences from the past subconsciously code the brain to protect the individual, leading to reactionary behaviours.
Often results in:	Friction, overreactions, mistrust

All of us come into a new position with all we are: the good, the bad, and everything in between. When we have gone through negative experiences or lived through a traumatic event, our brains become programmed to subconsciously scan for familiar situations or experiences in an effort to protect us from more pain. Once triggered, it fires off the alarm, telling us, "Oh no!

Here it comes again!" Whether we're actually in danger or not becomes irrelevant.

For example, imagine someone being in a car accident. Let's say they stopped at a red light, and the car behind them *didn't*. They then had to go through the process of dealing with insurance and getting their car repaired. Maybe they even had to deal with neck and back pain for a prolonged period. Years later, when they sit in the passenger seat on a road trip with friends, they may get nervous as they approach a stop sign and see a car rapidly approaching in their rearview mirror. Their shoulders scrunch up to their ears as they keep checking the rearview mirror, hoping the car will stop, maybe even putting their own foot on the imaginary brake on the floor. They may not realize at the moment that these responses are a direct result of their past pain.

Or imagine if someone felt like they never had enough money as a child. Their parents probably constantly said things like, "Money doesn't grow on trees," or "No—that's a waste of money." Then as an adult, when their teenager brings home a flyer about an international school trip, they glance at the amount and immediately say no. Despite their teen's enthusiasm for the experience, they mentally shut down and claim it's too expensive, even if they know they can afford it.

The issue here is that triggers don't come with warning signs. They just show up when you least expect, and the reactions they set off can lead to real damage—even if the danger itself was imagined. The internal protective instinct of the brain follows its own logic based on past pain, but the external behaviours experienced may appear illogical in the present context.

The above examples give us an idea of what it can look like in our personal lives. But what about the damage it causes in the workplace?

The blind spots for our leaders in this chapter were the results of some past pain. They were subconsciously reacting to fears developed over time from various painful experiences. From the fear of being excluded, to the fear of losing a job, to the fear of not being heard, these leaders had to shift *away* from the fear that was creating friction in their lives toward faith—in themselves and in their teams.

 ## Connie: The Connector

After working in a large firm, Connie had recently decided to start a specialized law firm with two other partners. They were thrilled to have her on their team because she had a phenomenal reputation as a brilliant lawyer in their market. Beyond this, she was also a bestselling author, an incredible communicator, and a renowned speaker for her clients in the financial sector.

Connie has a strong brand based on her deep expertise in creating contracts and legal agreements to mitigate risk. She can command the attention of thousands of people at a time during her speaking events and always receives positive feedback from participants.

Offstage, she's also top-notch in helping clients set up legal structures so they can have clarity about where their responsibilities begin and end. Within the financial industry, she's become a sought-after defence attorney for high-stakes cases when her clients are being sued. In short, saying she has a successful brand and practice feels like quite the understatement.

The first thing I noticed about Connie when I met her was how she genuinely *loves* people. Her personality radiates warmth and welcome for everyone she comes into contact with. She makes a point of taking the time to get to know people on a personal level, and her ability to be present makes you feel like you're the most important person in the world.

She understands the impact of a thoughtful gift, like a scented candle, a handwritten note, or even an invitation to dinner. Once Connie "adopts" you, it feels like you've gained a new friend who is always there for you. There's truly no better nickname for her than the "Connector."

Then one day, Connie learned a talented lawyer at her firm had decided to quit, and during their exit interview with the HR department, they mentioned how they didn't exactly enjoy working with her. They stopped short of saying she was the primary reason for them leaving, but still listed it as *one* of their reasons. This information *tortured* Connie!

Her partners and HR department didn't think It was all that serious—they saw the lawyer's exit as just one of those "not a good fit" situations and suggested she brush it off and not take it to heart. Connie, on the other hand, felt she had to act immediately. Her first instinct was to reach out to a coach and learn how to be a better boss.

This makes her pretty unique from many of the other situations we've covered because she initiated the coaching process for *herself.* Even when others discouraged her, she sensed the presence of a blind spot. She didn't know what it was yet, but she was committed to addressing it and knew she couldn't do it alone.

When I interviewed her colleagues and direct reports, many of the impact statements praised her compassion for team members and clients and her poise and confidence at speaking engagements. They also mentioned her loyalty as a strength they admired and appreciated.

But when she was out of her comfort zone, they noted her stress levels rose, and then all bets were off.

One stakeholder described the contrast in behaviour this way:

"When Connie is time-pressed or stressed, her communication style changes significantly. She can become abrupt, impatient, have trouble listening without interrupting, and her tone can be very sharp. This makes the other person feel bad and even disrespected. This can damage the tremendous goodwill that she creates with others."

Feedback also indicated how, although it seemed like she was listening, Connie often forgot what was said and had to be reminded. Some stakeholders came to her defence on this, justifying her forgetfulness as a symptom of how busy she was. They admitted how difficult it must be to remember every detail when she had so much going on at once. But others pointed out this was still another sign she was stressed and distracted.

Those who worked one-on-one with Connie really loved learning from her directly and asked for more mentorship opportunities. They observed how, when she was working within her zone of genius, she was incredible to watch. But they also noticed how when a task pushed her out of her comfort zone, her anxiety increased, and her mood changed drastically.

Team members indicated they could tell if she was feeling stressed by the quality of the emails she sent. If they were clear and concise, she was having a good day. When she let her stress levels get the best of her, emails became fragmented and confusing, lacking the context for them to complete tasks efficiently, prompting more back-and-forth emails for clarification.

I also noticed an element of distrust showing up in our sessions together. Connie would create false assumptions when she was triggered, claiming people were "working against her" or "waiting for her to fail." These kinds of nefarious projections created concern for her team when they felt like she didn't trust them to do their jobs. Furthermore, they felt like this distrust was keeping them from getting new opportunities or more control over the tasks they were assigned.

Thankfully, having the self-awareness to ask for coaching kept Connie open to all this feedback and willing to take it all in stride.

One of the first revelations for Connie was realizing how critical she could be about herself. Digging deeper, she felt this was rooted in her complicated relationship with her mom. From a young age, Connie consistently blamed herself for her mother's behaviours rather than recognizing the flaws in her mom. She paid more acute attention to the dialogue in her head and noticed that whenever she moved out of her zone of genius to a place of stress, her thoughts sounded more and more like her mom judging her.

Long story short, this "mom voice" in her head was causing a trauma response for her. When Connie understood this trigger's power to strip away her confidence, she learned to remind herself that her team believed in her. With this mental trick, she could then silence her inner critic.

Although it may seem odd how one employee leaving the firm would make her feel so insecure about her leadership, her brain felt betrayed by this person. She even compared it to the rejection she felt when she went through her divorce while her children were young. She had committed to a lifetime with someone who then let her down, which caused her to feel rejected and isolated and to question whether she could trust anyone—including herself.

Connie came to the conclusion that her lack of faith in herself and her fear of rejection were causing her to be overly reactive with her team members. Her projection of past hurts was inadvertently causing her even more pain in the present.

In fact, her brain's lack of trust was evident in her personal relationship outside of work too. Her boyfriend was an amazing person, but she couldn't bring herself to take a leap of faith and move their relationship to the next level.

The real subconscious reasons for her actions were beginning to move into her conscious decisions. The need to avoid rejection was of utmost importance to this Connector, and it was time to make the changes necessary so her intentions (to be close to people) matched her decisions, actions, and impact on others.

One key strategy we used was discussing the concept of acting on faith or fear. When she felt triggered, her feelings of inadequacy and the fear of losing connection with someone would rise up, and she'd dive into fight mode. But if she slowed down by using breathwork techniques and took a moment to consider the *faith* she had in herself and her peers, she could shift away before plunging into a negative emotional state.

Another strategy we put into place was taking advantage of her talent as a negotiator in the context of litigation and reframing those skills to her interactions with others. In typical negotiation scenarios, it was all about getting as much as she could. But she realized that when it came to running a partnership, it was more about maximizing the output of the workforce. This meant her role was to inspire, empower, and cultivate a positive environment for everyone else.

She started to notice the value in taking the time to express gratitude for her team members. Furthermore, she communicated their strengths in reference to the tasks she assigned, showing them that she trusted their judgment and had their backs when they needed support and mentorship —which led to better performance from them.

Bringing consciousness to her triggers from past pain helped her practice mindfulness to see she could have more peace and happiness in her life. We talked about the "trust switch" in her brain and how hers had a tendency to get flipped to "distrust" mode too quickly. Keeping it on the "trust" setting (presuming the individual's trustworthiness) while taking the time to intently listen to others helped her to build empathy. From there, she could deepen the relationships she loved to create so much and experience the connection she thrives on as a Connector.

Using our time together as a springboard into a more peaceful approach to leadership, Connie was able to strengthen those connections with her team and in her personal life. She trusts her team with bigger opportunities, and they know they can come to her for advice when they need it. When faced with a judgmental opinion, she is now better equipped to empathize with the other person's point of view rather than taking it on and overreacting. I'm also happy to say that Connie chose to trust her heart and commit to moving in with the man she loved to further deepen her most important relationship outside of work.

 ## Paul: The Protector

Being responsible for protecting a multibillion-dollar company with hundreds of thousands of employees from corruption and ensuring government compliance in over 120 countries is a huge undertaking—and Paul doesn't take the responsibility lightly. Paul is the one who proactively establishes his company's compliance processes and supports IT infrastructure to keep everything up and running with integrity. Only a handful of people in the world can do what he does on such a large scale.

When he's not doing all of that, he also educates team members across the globe so that they are aware of corporate compliance and how it looks within their different roles. Paul is a natural-born storyteller with an authentic enthusiasm for helping people understand corporate compliance issues, so he transforms typically dull compliance content into compelling and memorable lessons for his "audience." By using carefully crafted cliffhangers and metaphors blended with his charisma, Paul stimulates people's consciences to act ethically and with integrity in the workplace.

Furthermore, Paul truly cares about the organization. His empathy and kindness manifest throughout his teams in the form of friendships that go beyond a typical working relationship. With his love of creating strong bonds and his values for integrity and protecting the company, I've dubbed Paul the "Protector."

Since starting with the company, Paul has made an incredible difference in reducing the number of major incidents and protecting the organization. When I spoke with one key stakeholder, it was obvious how much people valued him. They were impressed with his functional leadership and his relationships with his team members.

However, they were also concerned they wouldn't be able to retain him if they had to continually make excuses for the way he interacted with other executives. One stakeholder shared his viewpoint on the way Paul let the stress of his job affect his performance:

"On Paul's best day, he collaborates very well and gets feedback from others to calibrate moving forward in a measured way. On a less-great day, he can be perceived as imposing or powering ahead at the expense of listening and collaborating with others."

Team members praised Paul's enthusiasm and passion, but they also pointed out that he needed to take more opportunities to listen to others' ideas and suggestions. He had a tendency to get frustrated easily and needed to demonstrate more patience. Although people understood challenging circumstances and resource constraints made his job difficult, they felt Paul needed to find ways to handle the stress more effectively rather than openly complaining. When he'd begin a rant, his emotions would get the best of him, creating tension capable of damaging important relationships.

Many times, as we were going over the impact statements, I'd hear him say, "Oh, this is going to get me fired." He seemed quite stressed, so I had to keep reminding him that there were also many positive comments in addition to the opportunities for improvement. The latter seemed to be stealing his attention, so I had to reassure him no one was talking about firing him. The pros of keeping his talent on staff overwhelmingly outweighed any thought of letting him go. I assured him that by keeping an open mind and making a few tweaks here and there, he'd become recognized as an even better leader and contributor to the company.

Additional feedback suggested Paul showed up as a one-stop shop of information for others. He ran meetings like it was a solo performance, hampering other team members from providing their input and blocking collaboration with important stakeholders. They suggested that Paul should encourage more dialogue with other executives as this could lead to a better understanding of where they were coming from, which could lead to more cordial agreements.

We began our coaching by discussing his role as the Protector of the company and acknowledging how huge of a responsibility it was. It became obvious how much stress he was holding. He felt vulnerable due to the risk his job entailed. For example, he would panic if someone in South America wasn't following a process he'd put in place, fearing he would get blamed for their actions—and then fired.

In light of the inherent risk in his role, it became totally normal for his brain to hit the "panic button" a little too often, leading him to assume the worst when confronted with an issue. But there had to be a way for him to understand that a simple alignment issue wasn't cause for overreaction and harsh judgment. For Paul to protect his own health and ability to influence his organization in a positive manner, we needed to build some mechanisms for his brain *not* to freak out so easily.

Over the course of our coaching conversations, Paul eventually shared how he had been let go from his two previous positions over how he had handled conflict with his leadership. So, his brain wasn't totally panicking for no reason—he had painful experiences from his past that had created this particular trigger.

What I so often see with triggers from past pain is how the brain's desire to protect us results in fear—and then fear triggers self-sabotaging behaviours because we can't think straight. In my opinion, the bigger issue for Paul was not the fear of being fired but his fear of being *judged*. This fear was leading him to repeat old behaviours. In an effort of self-preservation, he'd get frustrated, which would only create tension and make things worse.

For example, sometimes he had to go into meetings to explain how the company was out of compliance. His anxiety would then spike because he couldn't report that everything was sunshine and roses. Even though the meeting was intended to solve the problem, he'd jump in and judge the other executives before they could have the opportunity to critique him. It was as though his brain was saying, "The best defence is a strong offence." But then he'd panic and start to spiral, knowing this same behaviour is what had gotten him in trouble in the past.

At this time, Paul was reaching a milestone with his company. He was about to be at this firm longer than any other in his past. This was both good news and bad news for Paul. The good news was that he built a great track record and proven his value. The bad news was that he increasingly wanted to protect his reputation and not let anything wreck it.

Yes, he'd made it pretty far this time around, but he felt like time was running out on a bomb. Between the challenges he was facing due to his triggers and the feedback he was receiving, he could see people were unhappy—and it was because of him. He had become "the bad news guy." He couldn't help but imagine that at any moment, he'd be out looking for his next job.

His brain was filled with negative predictions that, if left unaddressed, would become self-fulfilling prophecies. He was developing a negative persona that was hindering his natural ability to give inspirational speeches and gain an authentic followership through trust.

Paul needed to get to a place where he had confidence in his abilities and talent. At speaking events, he had a way of projecting a sense of openness rather than defensiveness, which made people feel like they could be honest about their situations and receive judgment-free support from him. If he could do this in front of a large group, he was also capable of doing so when handling challenges in smaller meetings.

Instead of thinking *I'm the "bad news guy" who needs to enforce the rules and rub people the wrong way*, he shifted to thinking *I'm the "good news guy" who listens, makes positive assumptions about people's intentions, and creates trusted collaborations to inspire compliance."*

Rather than presuming the worst about people, Paul engaged his curiosity. He worked to understand others' perspectives and to see how they were trying to do the right thing and weren't trying to ignore his policies or subvert him. He modeled this by showing he was open to working with them individually to resolve issues because he had good faith that they weren't trying to get away with murder.

Before we met, many people were afraid to confront Paul with the truth whenever they spotted a business risk because, even though they knew he would find a solution, they would rightfully predict that he would weaponize their transparency and make *them* look bad. He realized during our work together that whenever he remained approachable, confident, and poised, people were much more trusting and forthcoming with potential risks and became comfortable reaching out to him to prevent incidents.

As a result, people started calling him for consultations before making decisions. He loved this new proactive approach because he saw how it caused his anxiety levels to drop. It also retrained his brain to not switch to "panic mode" so quickly. Paul now takes a moment before walking into meetings to set his own intentions. He affirms to himself, "I'm going to seek alignment by listening and being curious."

As a Protector, Paul also tended to "protect" his team from having to deal with some of the hardest work. But through this process, he also learned to trust them and delegate more of his work their way, freeing him up for some much-needed leisure. He was able to insert time for writing, which recharges him during the weekends, and he's become quite the prolific writer!

Moving from judgment to openness and presumption to curiosity has helped him become an even better leader at work and in his daily life. He's not worried about how others perceive him. The company continues to scale up; even his wife has said she loves the "new Paul." His self-fulfilling prophecy of infuriating people and then losing his job came to an end when he let go of the fear he had carried as a trigger from past pain. He now has faith that the changes he's made will continue to contribute to his success in his company for years to come.

 ## Mary: The Marketer

Growing up in a military family, Mary was born and raised in India. After graduating from university, she began working for a large US-based technology company that had established an offshore office in her city. She was ambitious and recognized as a top performer, so once she gained enough experience, she was offered a position to relocate to North America, where she stayed for another fourteen years.

As she rose up the ranks, she loved the culture at work. After all, the hierarchical structure in the company felt familiar to her family's military background. She thrived, earning promotions through her work ethic and intelligence. Although she loved her time at this firm, she was eventually recruited away by one of their clients because of how much they loved working with her.

At this new company, Mary was taken aback by what we'll call "corporate culture shock." The structure there was a stark contrast to what she'd been used to, and after a few years, she decided to move on. She tried a couple of other companies afterward but struggled to get the recognition she felt she deserved and had enjoyed at her first employer. I met her shortly after she had joined her latest employer and had been there for about a year.

Mary was a strong, commercially savvy leader who got results with the clients. She had been hired as a sales leader for one of their largest divisions and made an impression with her new company by bringing in big clients quickly. Mary was assertive, and they loved how she wasn't afraid to jump in and tell potential clients what they were missing out on and exactly what they needed. Mary demonstrated how she was the "Marketer" because of her ability to market both herself and her organization to earn the client's confidence and gain success.

Mary was also focused on marketing herself internally. In her first company, there had been clear accountability lines, so she had learned to create visibility around her contributions so she would be rewarded for her work. She took ownership of her assigned territory and was able to drive results with a high degree of autonomy, which made it easy to advocate for her advancement.

Within her latest company, though, it took a team of cross-functional peers with different specializations to close deals of such great magnitude, which clashed with Mary's independent drive. She continued her strategy of creating visibility for her work through a habit of making sure leadership *knew* what deals *she* was closing. But this approach wasn't landing very well. Her leadership knew Mary couldn't be landing these deals on her own, so they were skeptical about her ability to be a team player.

The CEO reached out to me because he thought Mary would benefit from coaching to help her with her integration. He could see she required some support in adjusting to their work culture. Simply put, he felt that her constant self-promotion wasn't sitting well specifically with the rest of the team who worked on the deals with her. It hadn't taken long for people to dislike working with Mary, given her reputation for taking all the credit and not showing any kind of appreciation for the hard work of her peers or their teams. She also clashed with some team members when she referred to them as "staff," making them feel like they were ranked lower than she was.

Many stakeholders reported how Mary created confusion because she didn't openly share what she was learning from her client contacts. Instead, she would keep important information to herself and give team members directives without telling them the context of why specific tasks were required or explaining their relevance. She'd simply say they came from discussions she'd had with the clients, and any other information was confidential. Doing so seemed to provide a subconscious form of protection and pride, giving her the sense of having "top secret" information that gave her an upper hand, making her more valuable to the company.

As a result, her internal team felt like Mary was more aligned with the client than her colleagues, and that she didn't see them as worthy of her trust. This Marketer's superpower with client-facing interactions was sabotaging her relationships with team members internally. One stakeholder shared the following:

> *"When Mary first arrived, it was probably important for her to communicate her competencies and experience as well as demonstrate that she has a strong external network that respects her. Everyone sees that now, so it is no longer necessary for her to continue to communicate that."*

In other words, she needed to move away from self-promotion and think more about contributing to a healthy team dynamic. One suggestion for improvement was that it would be great for Mary to start using her natural gifts as a Marketer to promote *other* people on her internal teams by giving them credit and finding ways to show them appreciation.

Mary confirmed that the past pain of feeling unappreciated and unrecognized at her former companies made her feel subconsciously compelled to promote herself. It was like she was a broken record, playing a song about her own strengths and worthiness, day in and day out. In doing so, this trigger from past pain was blinding her to the pain of unappreciation she was inflicting on others.

Once she understood that the company saw her strengths without her continuously needing to point them out, Mary began addressing her subconscious fear of not being seen. She accepted it was time to consciously trust that if she lifted up her team and expressed their success, the leadership would automatically include her in the celebration too.

Going back to her family's military background, she realized she could embrace this idea of everyone rising up together to share the spotlight. She did some mental rewiring around her interactions with leadership. During update discussions, she focused more on praising individual team members and even giving others the opportunity to lead meetings and share their insights. Mary started to see that it was in her best interest to celebrate her team's success, bragging about their accomplishments to give them the visibility she used to crave only for herself.

As a Marketer, she recognizes the power of words and how choosing the right words is imperative to a successful campaign. So how did it translate into her interactions with people? No more calling them the "staff!" She intentionally modified her vocabulary to avoid words with abrasive and controlling connotations. She deliberately developed a much more inclusive communication style and promoted the greatness of the entire team.

By creating an atmosphere where everyone felt appreciated, she herself felt more comfortable and interested in hearing more from her team members. She started to elicit their feedback and notice their individual expertise so she could be more precise in marketing the company's capabilities to her clients. She even created situations where she could get to know her team members on a personal level with get-togethers at her home.

In the same way that a good marketing campaign compels the audience to take action, this Marketer learned to cultivate a culture of inspiration over directives. Now people are *inspired* to work on her team and have learned how to elevate one another from her example. It's a beautiful thing to behold, indeed!

The Takeaway

In all three case studies here, my clients had recently joined new companies, which probably isn't a coincidence when we think about triggers from past pain. Career changes are often fraught with anxiety, and our brains are particularly attuned to *not* repeating any mistakes from the past.

I have noticed in my work that three different "gremlins" plague almost all executives in the first eighteen months or so of taking on a new role at a new organization. I find it helps to warn my clients about these gremlins because at least if they know they exist, they can keep an eye on them.

The three gremlins come in the form of three basic questions:

1. "Am I adding enough value?"

2. "Am I being valued?"

3. And finally, "Did I make a mistake choosing to work here?"

The three questions and their corresponding cloud of uncertainty makes integrating executives highly sensitive to being noticed, appreciated, and recognized—which can then bring out a number of agitating behaviours.

These three gremlins exist because the leader *wants* to do a great job, but the uncertainty and fear of repeating past mistakes creates a gap between their intentions as a leader and the impact of their behaviours. Instead, we have to choose to manage our gremlins by becoming curious about our behaviours. Usually, this means we have to name the past pain that was triggered and make the conscious decision to deal with it. This helps us move forward in a positive direction.

I like to think of triggers as these big red buttons hiding out in our bodies. And once they get pushed—look out! A trigger creates a temporary involuntary emotional state. We need to examine the button and disconnect it, so the negative behaviours associated don't explode out of us.

Connie learned to treat the trigger as the enemy rather than blame other people and disconnect from them. By quieting her fear of losing people, she has strengthened her ability to create authentic connections in work and life. Paul was able to throw out his old "I'm going to get fired" panic button and saw how his fears of being judged by others diminished. He found it's easier to let go of judging others when you aren't worrying about being judged. And Mary continues to elevate her team members by quieting the trigger that used to scream that she needed to prove herself. As they find success working together on large-scale deals, she understands her own value without having to constantly remind others of her value. And when her team celebrates big wins, it's a win for her too.

No way around it—dealing with past pain *hurts*. But it's necessary for leaders to heal both themselves as individuals and their relationships with others. We can ignore a broken, displaced bone, but unless it is put back in place, it won't heal properly. This will then negatively affect our entire body over time, infecting other areas or leaving us with a permanent limp. We can leave our reactive behaviours in our subconscious and hobble forward as leaders until we're too broken to function, or we can dig into the depths to consciously heal. Only then can we come out on the other side, ready for the next marathon.

TRIGGERS FROM PAST PAIN

Our leaders here were completely unaware of how their past pain was still affecting their present actions, but becoming aware of their triggers empowered them to be proactive rather than reactive.

Everyone has past pain, so learning to identify and recognize those pains is essential in taming the triggers that come along with them. Sometimes our behaviours don't properly portray the outcomes we truly desire or the mindsets we know we should have. For example, Mary was focused on proving herself in the way most of us would expect a junior employee to behave rather than a seasoned veteran of her standing. This theme of misalignment in our mindsets will be the final blind-spot area we will tackle together.

Summary

How triggers from past pain happen:	An old threat to your safety and security is no longer relevant, but you still have residual self-protection instincts.
The shift you need:	Recognize that you have a scar, but you are no longer under a threat and don't need to protect yourself.
Self-reflection questions to help you uncover triggers from past pain:	• What negative outcomes am I secretly afraid of and determined not to repeat? • Where have I been taken advantage of or wronged in the past that I need to prevent from happening again? • Where do I lack trust in myself, in others, or in my life circumstances? • Are there any specific events, words, or images/sounds which seem to send me off "the deep end"?

YOUR NOTES

....

....

....

....

....

....

....

....

....

....

....

....

....

....

....

....

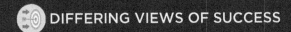

MISMATCHED MINDSETS

Simple definition:	Things people do or ways they behave which no longer match the role they are in.
Root cause:	People hold on to an old mindset that made them successful in a previous role, failing to evolve their way of thinking.
Results in:	Misprioritization, demotivation, lack of vision

While you progress through various roles and elevated levels of responsibilities in your professional life, your focus and competencies require continuous evolution. To help my clients with their development, our programs at Leaderley build leadership competencies in three specific areas: Leading Self, Leading Others, and Leading Change. Over the course of a career, each collective of competencies serves to direct a leader's intention and action. The leader's mindset also activates different values that determine their mindset and approach.

At the beginning of our careers, we find ourselves building up our foundational mindset of Leading Self, or rather, self-mastery if you prefer this term. That's to be expected! Think back to your earliest working days; you were probably directing about 80 percent of your energy toward leading yourself. This included learning the rules of the workplace, acquiring new skills, and sharpening your talents. As you gain confidence in your skills, you discover new ways to achieve your goals. Along the way, you let go of those "newbie" feelings and become a contributing member of the company.

The problem arises when leaders continue to operate from a Leading Self mindset as they elevate into more senior positions. For example, Mary the Marketer in our last chapter was exhibiting a more junior-oriented Leading Self mindset by being more focused on her individual achievement and self-promotion. Instead, she needed to elevate herself and shift her energy and focus to leading *others* and leading *change* in order to scale her impact.

Once you've mastered leading yourself, you're often offered the privilege of leading a team. Your perspective *must* therefore shift from leading yourself to effectively leading others. You will continue nurturing your Leading Self skillset, but the difference here is that your focus shifts to developing ways to add value to your entire team. There is a progression and transition along the spectrum from Leading Self to Leading Others. It might feel like a 40/60 split—40 percent focus on self, 60 percent on others.

Then the higher you rise, the percentage may change to 30/70 or 20/80, but it's always moving toward being *others-focused*.

When you're working from a Leading Others mindset, you're putting energy and time into collaboration and teamwork. This goes back to building your others-awareness so you can create strong connections with the people you rely on for success. The better the working environment you create, the more productivity and happiness you and your team can experience together. As you may recall, Lucas the Loyalist was amazing at this level with his departmental team, but when he was moved to the executive team, he initially struggled to evolve his view of Leading Others. Ultimately, he had to see the whole company as his team, which matured his mindset into one of Leading Change, where the entire company could benefit from his loyalty.

At this highest mindset level of Leading Change, you continue to work on yourself and leading others, but your career focus and values shift to making a difference in the world. These are the executives who know how to take care of themselves, are connected to the team in a healthy way, and are now focused on scaling their positive impact to leave behind a beautiful legacy.

At the point in your career where you are focused on Leading Change, you ask yourself—and your peers—how you can be of greatest influence and impact to the company *and* the world. Victoria the Visionary was striving to be at this level when we met. What kept her from reaching it was the simple fact that she hadn't mastered Leading Others. All it took was a little shift for her to include her team in the change she wanted to make in the world. Then they all leveled up to join the cause while developing their working relationships at the same time.

Mismatched mindsets happen when leaders continue to live with a mindset that may have helped them get to their current role instead of evolving their values to match the mindset they *need* to have. This gap in mindsets becomes a breeding ground for all kinds of blind spots, including all the ones we've already discussed. But if leaders can realign their mindset to match their level of influence, they can experience greater levels of success with their teams.

I developed a values assessment for this specific reason: to help my coaching clients uncover their mismatched mindsets and discover ways they can uplevel. By picking their top values and mapping these values against the levels of leadership, the data points to where their mindset may be mismatched. The assessment pulls the blindfold off and allows them to see how they can evolve their mindset, their values, and, therefore, their leadership.

With our final blind-spot area of mismatched mindsets, we're going to see how three leaders discovered this about themselves. They each had to find the misalignment between the expectations of their roles and their mindset. The work of realigning these was the fun part.

Chelsea: The Champion

When it comes to complex technology implementations, Chelsea is the best sales veteran in the market. Within the consulting company she works for, Chelsea's team has a better win rate than anyone else could expect to achieve. She has the expertise to understand how to best frame the solutions to meet the customer's needs, and her prowess in orchestrating flawless presentations and high-quality proposals makes it a no-brainer to call Chelsea the "Champion."

In terms of sales presentations, she is especially gifted at giving her team the information they need to build rapport and trust with the customers. Her instincts about what really matters to the customers help her hone proposals to speak specifically to their top priorities. Chelsea works hard to create a differentiated sales experience for each client as a way for her to communicate, "I see you, I hear you, and I can help you."

Chelsea had been a rock star in sales for over twenty years, and when we met, she had been with her current company for three years. She was brought in specifically to build their sales capability the same way she had done at other companies during her career.

And it seemed to be working! She immediately had an impact on their conversion and win rates. Customers were sharing fantastic feedback about how impressed they were with how things were going under her leadership. Everyone was excited about the actual outcomes she was driving... and yet Chelsea herself was internally frustrated and angry most of the time.

She was focused on the changes she still needed to make at the company. Three years in, she felt like she was pulling teeth to get everyone on board. As a Champion, losing wasn't an option for her. When things didn't go the way she wanted them to, she would feel really down. She couldn't just "brush it off" and move on.

As a result, a culture clash developed concerning how she presented herself as a leader. Her intensity was getting the best of her. You know the saying about "finding the silver linings in the cloud," right? Well, much of the feedback she received was about how she *never* talked about the silver lining because she was ultra-focused on all the dark parts of the cloud. One colleague even said this:

"Chelsea can find a dark cloud in the silver lining!"

Her style reminded me of a major league baseball coach who takes up coaching a Little League team. Instead of meeting the young players where they are and building on their existing strengths, the coach just points out all of their weaknesses and gets frustrated when the players can't immediately leap to pro-level expectations.

Part of the problem was that Chelsea had previously worked with a massively successful sales team. Although she was brought in to recreate that success, it would take time, kindness, and patience to get the new company's current team to perform at the high levels she was accustomed to. But this mindset wasn't in this Champion's playbook.

In fact, positive reinforcement just wasn't a part of her vocabulary. Chelsea was so focused on winning that she'd push hard for team members to get better at their jobs with little to no explanation as to *how* they could improve. Her only instruction was to tell them what *not* to do. As a result, people were feeling beaten down and defeated by her leadership approach.

Reading the impact statements was frustrating for Chelsea. She felt like the stakeholders were being ungrateful for everything she was trying to accomplish. From her perspective, all she had done was point out where the holes were in their performance. After all, this Champion had a proven track record of knowing how to get the wins—it's why she was hired! So, to her, it felt like the stakeholders were nitpicking.

She started by trying to be "nicer" to others. But because her motivation wasn't authentic, her "niceness" came across as passive aggressive. This was no real surprise, given that she was forcing herself to act a certain way to appease what she saw as her "sensitive" team members whose desire to win wasn't as high as her own.

It's important to note here that Chelsea's ability to lead herself was phenomenal. She'd spent over twenty years learning, developing herself, and perfecting client pitches. She was so attuned to their needs, clients almost felt like she was reading their minds. Every role she was asking her team members to take on was a role she'd perfected for herself in the past. But she wasn't seeing how she was trying to lead others from a mindset of Leading Self. Her mismatched-mindset blind spot was keeping her from accomplishing her goals—and the goals of her team members. She was creating her own roadblocks.

A big moment for her was the day she verbalized how miserable she felt at work. She hated feeling like she was constantly fighting and how it was wearing her down. She realized that she'd put herself on an impossible racetrack, running in circles, and she was miserable. Chelsea used to love the rush of dopamine she experienced after getting a win. But her unrelenting focus on how things "should be" better was over-shadowing the wins, creating a sense of dread for her. She was continuously looking back, dwelling on what could have been done for a better outcome.

We had to move her focus away from the outcome—win or lose—and redirect to whether she was creating an environment of inspiration, development, and positivity. Given her skills at

Leading Self, we focused on affirmations and meditations first. We considered questions like "Can you win in life without being happy? Can you win in collaboration if there are people who don't want to work with you? Can your team win if they are miserable along the journey?"

She developed an authentic curiosity for how work could be more fun. This newfound desire to find happiness at work helped her redefine the win beyond a commercial transaction. By reframing her main incentive of winning to one of enjoying her daily experience, Chelsea started to notice a shift in herself and how she saw her team. Rather than focus on the imaginary "future" state of the team, she learned to focus on the real progress they had made. Her mindset evolved.

Instead of being a solo Champion, Chelsea became her team's coach—but a coach with the heart of a cheerleader. She looked at their strengths and celebrated their expertise. Cocreation happened more regularly as she put herself "on the sideline," trusting her team to get onto the field and use what she'd taught them to get the win.

With her new mindset of Leading Others and her team responding well, she found she had more time to evolve into a mindset of Leading Change. Chelsea began thinking more strategically and created a five-year vision for her goals, which she shared with the CEO. And because she recognized that taking care of others required taking good care of herself, she doubled down on leading herself by revamping her self-care rituals. This included taking the time to re-evaluate and improve her personal habits at home, from meal planning to her exercise routine. In doing so, she discovered how improving her well-being outside work allowed her to bring her best self to work each day.

Chelsea's focus on shifting her mindset paid off as her team achieved their highest sales growth rate ever—and her highest performance review. Her leadership acknowledged her tremendous contribution and began the process for her candidacy to make partner. Chelsea was also healthier and happier than ever, realizing that the more she "Championed" taking care of herself, the better equipped she was to lead her team, and in the process, also lead the change her company needed.

 ## Greg: The Go-Getter

When I met Greg, he had been with the same manufacturing company for twenty years, which showed in his incredible business acumen and depth. But he was also personable, easy to talk to, and was known to champion the career progressions of others. Everyone admired the fact that he had started on the plant floor, worked his way up to senior leadership, and now oversaw multiple plants.

Customers and leadership alike praised Greg's outstanding communication skills. Whenever he hosted customers or people from government programs at the plants, they left impressed by his charisma and charm. His effortless wit and humor aided the company in receiving investment funds for expansion. People admired Greg's career ascension, so they often sought out his feedback, hoping he could give them some great advice. These are just a few of the many reasons why Greg is the "Go-Getter."

On top of all that, this particular Go-Getter loves to take the time to understand issues on a deep level by going directly to the technicians and learning from them firsthand. His mind for metrics and knowing the right levers to pull has helped the company boost its profit margins by strategizing and brilliantly shifting production tactics.

Greg's ability to analyze and ask the right questions gives the impression that there is no problem he can't help to solve. This is why Greg the Go-Getter was the go-to choice when the company needed someone to oversee a large expansion.

However, when it was announced Greg would return to a particular plant to lead them through the expansion effort, there were rumblings of discontent throughout the plant about this decision. Given Greg's strengths and reputation, this puzzled HR, the leadership team, and Greg himself.

Still, the executive leadership team felt strongly he was the right person for the job and wanted to proactively ensure a smooth transition for both Greg and the team at the plant. They brought me in to help him be successful and to unpack the surprising reactions to his return.

To his own credit, Greg was quite open when we met, saying he'd evolved a lot since his last stint at the plant, and maybe people just didn't know the real him. He was willing to learn and looked forward to our coaching program so he could do what was necessary to address people's concerns and win their favor.

During my interviews, the problem became rather obvious. One of the biggest issues the stakeholders agreed on was best summarized as "When you work for Greg, you are working for his agenda."

As a Go-Getter, Greg was absolutely looking toward the next level he could attain. He'd typically work at one role for about two to three years before being promoted. And yes, he'd helped people advance their own careers, but the stakeholder interviews revealed that they felt Greg was very strategic and political about those he chose to promote. There always seemed to be an angle of *self-promotion* attached to his choices. And if Greg didn't see how someone would directly benefit his own personal trajectory, it led to these individuals feeling ignored or unimportant. So, while he thought he was great at Leading Others, there seemed to be an angle of Leading Self latched on to *how* he chose to lead others.

In fact, as Greg worked with people at different plants, they felt like they were a part of his team—*until* he was promoted, and then they simply didn't hear from him anymore. One minute they were collaborating and solving problems together—and then he was just gone, moving on to bigger and better things, ceasing all contact. It made them feel *used.*

One stakeholder specifically mentioned how some initiatives in process were critical for resolving production issues at a plant Greg was about to leave. They had requested that he keep in touch with the incoming manager to help them complete those initiatives. But when Greg didn't circle back after he started his new role, the workers felt like he had abandoned them. For them, he proved he wasn't genuine about helping—unless there was something in it for him.

It quickly became apparent we needed to aim his Go-Getter strengths toward repairing relationships and showing authenticity in order to gain the followership he needed to successfully lead the plant expansion project. One impact statement became an especially important piece of advice as it mentioned that if Greg were to get promoted again, he'd have to shift to "being more influential and inclusive rather than directive and competitive with others."

Greg was very responsive to the feedback and willing to make changes. He discovered he had more of a controlling instinct than he'd ever realized. Furthermore, he admitted it was absolutely true that he was continuously positioning himself for the next level.

When he realized he was only solving for one stakeholder group—that is, his leaders and influencers—he started to consciously work toward showing *all* of his peers and direct reports how he cared about the relationships he could build with them. He recognized that to effectively lead them, he needed to create an environment where his team members felt genuinely happy for his presence rather than resisting his appointment.

We started by creating an inventory of little ways he could show his peers he cared about them. One item on the list was to speak up about the issues plant managers across the board were noticing. In meetings, Greg looked for opportunities to show people he heard them and cared about the problems they were facing in the plant. Then he would find a small step he could take *right away* to help provide solutions so workers on the plant floor felt heard and valued. Instead of beginning a discussion by sharing his opinion, he'd give people time to have an open discussion, then support their choices, and only step in to help when they asked. By taking a few small steps into the Leading Change mindset, he saw how making things better for everyone also made him a better leader.

Another way Greg began to build relationships was by writing out the names of all 120-plus people he worked with each week. Every day, he'd run down the list and ask himself, "Who needs a win today?" Then he'd go pick people to recognize, reward, or encourage so that week after week, more and more of his people experienced a win. Everyone started to feel like they were learning and growing in leaps and bounds with his Go-Getter support.

Greg really took our coaching sessions to heart, sharing his new insights with his peers, and even began showing a more vulnerable side of himself. He also eliminated his habit of joking about others and turned the focus of the jokes onto his own personal struggles with his family or mistakes he'd made. Seeing a more human side of Greg really helped people see he wasn't just some ambitious and invincible being without any perceivable flaws. This encouraged further openness among the team, which was an outcome of our coaching he hadn't expected.

During the pandemic, an especially trying time for the essential workers on the production floor, he tapped into his creativity to show how much he valued them. He used his Go-Getter mentality to make fun inventory trades with other businesses. As a result, his team benefited from surprise deliveries of fresh-baked bread, bags of potatoes, and more.

Greg's leadership mindset evolution really paid off. He was eventually promoted to VP of operations and now oversees multiple regions of plants. Mastering his ability to Lead Others and answering the call to Lead Change enabled him to lean into the potential his executive team always knew he was capable of.

Finding ways to show his essential workers he genuinely cared about them created an environment of mutual respect.

To this day, I love catching up with Greg as often as possible. He likes to remind me of some of our discussions and how they helped him grow from an ambitious plant manager to a legacy-minded enterprise leader. I can't wait to see where his leadership and ambition will take him next!

 ## Cedric: The Celebrity

Born and educated in the UK, Cedric had worked on almost every continent by the time I met him. With experiences in multiple countries in Asia, Europe, and North America, along with a stint in Australia, he had a wealth of international experience. Combine this with his lighthearted personality, desire to take risks, and consistent delivery of results, and he became one of the youngest partners ever promoted at the firm.

His British satire and sense of humor gave him an ability to light up a room, which made him fun to work with. He's extremely organized and engaging, known for asking thoughtful questions and listening deeply to the responses of others. For these attributes and the way he attracts attention in meetings, I've dubbed him the "Celebrity." Cedric embodied a movie-star persona as he happily traveled the globe, meeting with clients and seamlessly adapting to different cultures. He knew how to work a room, and his playful approach, blended with his intelligence and compassionate nature, made him a magnet for talent. As you can imagine, all those traits in one person created a really fantastic management consultant.

We started working together because he was up for yet another promotion, one of the most senior partner levels. His leadership team wanted to make sure Cedric was ready to take on the advanced responsibilities of the role, given how he was comparatively much younger than the other candidates. My role was to help mature his leadership style in preparation for the possible promotion.

I first met with Cedric over video in the middle of one of his trips around the world, and he was super enthusiastic. This Celebrity saw our coaching sessions as a "perk" that few people had the benefit of receiving. He wasn't sure how I could help him because he knew he was doing an amazing job, but he was ready to give it a try, nonetheless.

Like many Celebrities, Cedric was amazing at building his personal brand, and I got to learn a lot about his rapid growth within the company firsthand. I saw the value he provided to the company as he shared with me metrics about his year-over-year performance and glowing client testimonials. From the impact statements I collected, we saw feedback that reflected these successes, but there were also some great suggestions where stakeholders felt he had room to improve.

People generally appreciated his confidence and ambition but stated he could come across as overconfident and too focused on getting his next promotion. He was fun to work with, but they wanted more patience and understanding from him on projects. Specifically, his team wanted opportunities to learn *from* him and grow into new positions themselves. He had a tendency to be controlling and picky when it came to any presentation he viewed as part of *his* branding. This attitude left little room for other team members to build their own brand.

He was shaken to find that the stakeholders weren't all saying he was amazing at his job. He had spent the better part of fifteen years being promoted faster than anyone else, and for the first time in his life, he was hearing he may be hitting a ceiling. As a Celebrity, Cedric *craved* external attention, so he had seen the promotions and praise like his own personal paparazzi, validating him as valuable. He had moved up rapidly by leading himself and his team, yes, but it was time to move into the Leading Change mindset if he were to be successful with the responsibilities the next promotion would entail.

In the Leading Change mindset, leaders have to realize their stakeholder list is expanding, and they need to be able to solve for *all* of the individuals involved. For Cedric, this meant shifting away from focusing exclusively on his own metrics.

I saw this shift in him when he described a client event he hosted. He remembered being there and speaking, entertaining people, and getting laughs as the centre of attention. But then he realized he was taking up too much space. He was actually keeping himself from making meaningful connections by not giving his team the opportunities to highlight *their* areas of expertise. It was great to hear about this "in the moment" self-awareness and how he course-corrected in real-time.

He also recognized that he never had longer-term goals beyond the next promotion milestone. He was so used to moving up every few years that it was challenging for him to accept how more advanced positions would likely require him to *stay* in a role for a longer span. It was even more difficult for him to grasp how he could be motivated by his contribution regardless of whether it led to any recognition for himself.

One of my recommendations was for him to experiment with shifting his focus slightly by asking himself two self-reflection questions. First, "How do I maximize my contribution even if no one knows about it?" And second, "With whom should I initiate a conversation to get advice on how to increase my positive impact?" This second piece was particularly challenging for him because he'd always felt he needed to find all the answers on his own. He'd perceived asking for help as a sign of weakness.

The result of this shift was incredible for Cedric. For starters, he discovered he loved getting advice from others. He saw how it deepened his relationships and also equipped him with so many new ideas about ways he could contribute even more. He started to enjoy others more and find ways to team up and cocreate interesting experiences and projects.

What's most interesting about Cedric's story is how his leaders ultimately decided to delay his promotion for at least a year, given some economic challenges—and Cedric surprised himself because he wasn't really disappointed by this change in plans. The former version of Cedric would have been furious and embarrassed. But now, with a new mindset matched to his level, he was so engaged in his current role that it didn't bother him at all. Instead, he was being enriched by the projects he had taken on based on his leadership team's advice. He focused on enjoying his current role and finding more opportunities for growth across his existing client portfolios. He even told me he felt *internally* motivated for the first time in his career, seeing how he could grow with or without the promotion.

For the next year, he invested in getting more involved in regional leadership activities and taking on more accounts while leaning into more ways he could contribute. Cedric also teamed up more easily and was less competitive, even sharing revenue credit with key contributors on his team instead of focusing solely on his own metrics. This led him to promote some of his team members and get *them* into partnership roles. By elevating others, he elevated himself.

This shift in focus as a Celebrity expanded Cedric's contributions and convinced his leadership that he could lead at the next level—and after a year, he *did* receive his next promotion. By addressing his mismatched mindset, he had closer connections and enhanced his contributions, which made the promotion milestone all the sweeter.

The Takeaway

Have you ever watched a pair of dancers when it was difficult to see who was leading and who was following? If a leader has a mindset that doesn't match the phase of their career, it's like the dancers getting out of step with one another. There might be many stops and starts, missed cues, and injured toes, which can leave both dance partners a little frustrated and confused.

But when a leader has the right mindset matched to their role and their values reflect those expected in their role, they can successfully "lead" the dance. When they're in alignment, the dance is beautiful, and no one is stepping on anyone's toes. When practiced long enough, muscle memory takes control, making it look effortless.

Chelsea had to move away from her differing view of success and learn how to incorporate her strengths as a means to help others achieve success. This meant starting where they were and acknowledging their wins along the way. Furthermore, she had to recognize that losing a deal was a trigger from past pain, causing her to miss out on the other wins happening around her. When she learned to convert her mindset of Leading Self to

Leading Others, she was able to level up and find success in a new phase of her career. Great things happened once she embraced optimism and redefined winning for her team and herself.

When Greg moved beyond Leading Self to truly Leading Others by creating lasting relationships, it brought him into the Leading Change mindset. He had been totally unaware of an unhealthy detachment between himself and the plant staff, oblivious to the unconscious habits he had developed as a result. When he confronted these head-on, he discovered how bolstering others would bolster his success. In exposing his blind spots, his eyes were opened to how a properly matched mindset made his efforts more synergistic and co-creative.

Cedric also learned how the skills that had initially made him successful needed to change. His brain wanted to repeat a pattern of past success to get the same results, but these outdated core beliefs had backfired at a certain point in his career. He had to let go of the false assumption that everyone loved everything he did and learn to make genuine connections and relationships. By making the necessary changes, he was able to exhibit authentic leadership habits, which better prepared him for his next promotion beyond an ego boost.

As I mentioned before, I use a values assessment for each of my clients to help leaders identify where their mindsets might be mismatched early in the coaching process. It's amazing how this one exercise can also expose the other blind-spot areas we've discussed.

Ready and inspired to address your blind spots? This may sound impossible because you don't know what you don't know, right? Certainly, it's much easier to identify your blind spots when you have an open mind *and* some outside help. But you can begin the process on your own with some self-reflection.

In the next chapter, I will share more about how you can strengthen your self-awareness enough to start making changes. The more you practice, the more you'll be able to tap into your others-awareness. And then you're on your way to the next phase of your leadership journey.

If you're curious about where your mindset might be focused right now and how your values affect how you operate, **take my value assessment.**

You can access it for free with this QR code or go to https://su.vc/leaderleyvalues

Summary

How mismatched mindsets happen:	Your behaviours, motivations, and values aren't matched with the level of your role.
The shift you need:	Shift your mindset and values to the appropriate place for your career level.
Self-reflection questions to help you uncover mismatched mindsets:	• What personal ambitions am I striving for? • Am I helping others or only helping myself? • What collaboration and culture do I want for my teams? • What is supposed to be my purpose? • Given my role, where should my focus be?

YOUR NOTES

....
....
....
....
....
....
....
....
....
....
....
....
....
....
....

 INTRODUCTION

BLIND SPOTS

 FALSE ASSUMPTIONS

 **UNHEALTHY DETACHMENT**

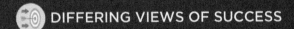 DIFFERING VIEWS OF SUCCESS

 OUTDATED CORE BELIEFS

 UNCONSCIOUS HABITS

TRIGGERS FROM PAST PAIN

MISMATCHED MINDSETS

 UNCOVERING BLIND SPOTS

CONCLUSION

UNCOVERING BLIND SPOTS

The How

By now I hope you feel ready to accept that throughout your entire career, blind spots will continue to appear. They aren't stagnant. They morph, mutate, and disguise themselves in new ways. At first, they might even be perceived as a strength, but unless you discover the shadow cast by your strength, you will inevitably bump into something due to your blind spot. I have found that as you make your way through your career and your life, your blind spots will reveal themselves to you—usually when you get curious because you have bumped into a new ceiling.

But take heart! This is a great way to know when it is time to improve your leadership. I want you to realize that when you bump against one of these glass ceilings, it is a chance to break through it.

**When you bump up against a glass ceiling,
it is a chance to break through it.**

Often, we are unaware of what attributes or behaviours cause the barrier we're facing. Uncovering your blind spots helps you break through more effectively and quickly.

Now that we've discussed each blind-spot area and received an insider's view for some of the ways they can manifest, let me check in on you: How are you feeling? Were there some blind spots that triggered you more than others? Did you recognize some of the people you work with (or even yourself) within some of the different case studies? Have you become a little more curious about your potential blind spots that may be the root cause of your struggles?

Here's the good news: you can start uncovering the blind spots within yourself and your organization *proactively and immediately*. I cannot stress this enough: Why not help *everyone* on your team uncover their blind spots? As you've seen in the case studies, when one person makes conscious changes, the positive impact on the organization multiplies.

You may be wondering what you can do to identify and address the blind-spot areas for your team in real time. Well, more good news: the information you require to close those pesky gaps between intention and impact is at your disposal. You just need to go get it! In this final chapter, I provide my suggestions for gathering the clues that can lead you to spotting the blind spots in your environment, along with a quick reference guide for self-reflection.

Culture

First and foremost, blind spots aren't just an individual issue—they're really a cultural issue. Great leaders create a culture of curiosity and humility that recognizes the process of uncovering blind spots as a core piece of professional development.

Think about it like this: When you learn how to drive, they don't teach you to check your blind spots *after* a collision, right? No, because then it's already too late. Instead, you're taught to check your blind spots when contemplating a turn or changing lanes.

Change often triggers blind spots—for better or worse. Change in a job role. Change in performance. Change in the economy, corporate structure, or mission. All are opportunities to find blind spots to safely navigate the change—or ignore them and invite a collision.

That's why making this kind of authenticity and vulnerability the norm is important. When team members prepare for a new role or put their name in the hat for the next promotion, why not provide them with the tools to check in on both their self-awareness and others-awareness?

When checking your blind spots becomes the norm, when it's encouraged and practiced *before* anyone makes their next move, everyone has the opportunity to share constructive feedback, learn from one another, and grow stronger relationships. This, in turn, creates a stronger organization that becomes more flexible and adaptable because people acquire the skills to change lanes without collisions.

The first step in preparing your team to discover their blind spots is to help them get *excited* about asking their key stakeholders (supervisors, peers, employees, and even clients) for feedback. This can be a daunting task because of the vulnerability required. To be ready, they need to be open to the possibility that there are a number of different truths they will have to face.

I find that the parable of the blind men and the elephant can be a helpful analogy to prepare them.

The parable goes like this: A group of blind men who have never heard of an elephant approach one. They each feel a different part of the elephant's body. As they each describe their observations based on their limited experience of the elephant, they share vastly different perceptions. Is it a tree? A fan? A snake?

This parable points out our tendency to claim absolute truth based on the limitations of our own beliefs and experiences while ignoring the experiences of others, which are equally valid and true. Likewise, uncovering your blind spots requires you as a leader to evolve to where you can be fully open to receive guidance from another human being's version of the truth with grace, dignity, and humility. Not only because it's the "right" thing to do but because you see the value in understanding your impact on others.

Data (Feedback) Collection

Guess what! The information you need to uncover blind spots is already available to you. The only problem is that it lives in *other people's minds,* which means you have to go get it. There will be clues, in feedback that you may have already received from them. And you can get access to more just by asking, but I want you to ask for it in the form of impact statements.

Great leaders ask those who experience their work and actions firsthand to share about the impact they are having on them. Likewise, you have a chance to set an example for your team by keeping an open mind and fearlessly collecting first-person feedback. I encourage my clients to treat feedback collection like a scientist treats data rather than relying on anonymous 360-degree surveys. The best way to get feedback is to do so *directly*.

The starting point is getting feedback from your stake-holders; that is, the individuals most affected by your intentions and actions. But remember, they can only share your impact on *them*. They often don't clearly understand your intention and may be even less capable of identifying your specific actions causing a suboptimal impact on them or the organization. They can sense the presence of a blind spot but can't tell you *how* it got there or how to *stop* it. The process begins with data collection followed by self-reflection.

When I help people find, define, and fix their blind spots, it starts by collecting and processing all the feedback they have received. As you've seen throughout our journey, my clients are very senior in their organizations and therefore can quickly identify around eight to eighteen individuals they have a significant impact on. The list generally includes direct reports, peers, supervisors and/or board members. To supplement the feedback they have already collected, I often meet with those stakeholders to collect what I refer to as *impact statements.*

The distinction between standard feedback and *impact statements* is their subjectivity. Feedback is often full of advice and preferences of the other party, including how they think their colleague should behave. Impact statements provide observations and examples from witnesses on their colleague's positive *and* negative effects on them personally.

This approach allows the stakeholders to express how my client affects them. They're asked, "Can you provide an example where this leader impacted you? How do you see their behaviours or actions positively and negatively impacting the team and organization?" I ask them to back their statements up with as many *specific* examples as possible.

What supports this level of transparency is one important promise that I make to my clients: 360-degree feedback remains *nonevaluative.* There is no scoring, only suggestions to be used in our coaching bubble. It can be tempting for client sponsors to want to use this data for performance conversations, but this is a red flag for me. If you want people to welcome this process and seek out the data they need to uncover and address their blind spots, you need to create appropriate safety around it.

That is why I embed collecting impact statements at the start of my coaching programs. It is an ideal way to kick off my six-step coaching process. When leaders are enrolled in a coaching program it gives us appropriate time to capture and unpack their blind spots because we typically work together for six to twelve months. Why so long? Because as you've seen, behaviour change requires *rewiring* the mind, which takes time.

The six steps to the Leaderley coaching programs are:

1. Collect impact statements from key stakeholders.

2. Discern key opportunity areas to improve the client's impact.

3. Explore intention with my client to understand the gap.

4. Identify the blind spots hiding in the gap that are causing the unintended result, missed opportunities or damage.

5. With new awareness of these blind spots, consciously modify and experiment with applying their strengths and learning new behaviours that better align intention with impact.

6. Monitor what works best for the client and their stakeholders and repeat the modified behaviour until it is fully embedded in their leadership style.

At the end of step six, the brain itself has been rewired, leading to new outcomes and lasting transformation.

Suffice it to say, my clients who undergo this process are incredibly brave. Not just the executives I am coaching but also the stakeholders. Although there is an opportunity for the stakeholders to remain anonymous, I encourage them to go on record and share attributed feedback as much as possible, because it *vastly* improves my client's ability to act on it. When stakeholders share their impact statements openly, it enables my client to ask for clarification to uncover their blind spots and request real-time feedback on their progress throughout the coaching engagement. This is very valuable.

In the absence of attributed feedback, I find my clients can't help themselves from guessing who said what—and they almost always guess wrong. They often attribute all of the positive comments to people they like, and all of the critical comments to those with whom they have weaker relationships. Unfortunately, doing so makes it harder for them to take accountability for making positive changes in their behaviour to address their blind spots. When they are able to see exactly who said what, it motivates them to improve *all* of their collaborations.

Attributed feedback is most powerful when it comes to impact statements, with specific examples of an individual's strengths *and* areas for improvement expressed within the full context of actual events. If you want to accelerate your people's understanding of how others perceive them, critical to spotting their blind spots, I suggest courage over caution for all parties involved in the coaching process.

That being said, in contexts where the feedback *needs* to remain anonymous, some data is better than no data, and I'm happy to support my clients in collecting the data in whatever form is available.

I facilitate collecting confidential information via interviews to capture key themes and Leaderley has built applications to collect written responses. Unlike conventional 360 surveys with actual comments being anonymously transposed into a report, we manually review the responses and create a customized report organized into key themes with supporting descriptions.

I find it important to avoid sharing direct responses because this generally causes clients to get too focused on individual responses and respondents to be too cautious about what they share. If respondents feel they need to protect their own anonymity, they provide much more vague information lacking examples and context in an attempt to protect the source. This makes it difficult for the leader to get value out of the survey results.

Because capturing feedback in an interview or customized 360 can be costly, Leaderley developed its automated version FeedbackFriend that collects and consolidates the key development themes using AI. The Leaderley application enables anyone to request feedback and makes it possible for respondents to share rich feedback so that the context is clear and can feel confident that only development themes will be shared with the leader.

I believe that getting feedback is **the most important leadership development activity a leader can do,** which is why I created this free resource that enables you to request anonymous feedback for yourself and receive consolidated themes so you can take action.

 Use this QR code or go to FeedbackFriend.ai and **give it a try** for free.

Synthesizing the Feedback

It's beautiful to work with teams who are open-minded about taking on unfiltered feedback from one another. It is such an honour to witness the shifts that can happen when a client embraces the impact statements without feeling judged or attacked because they understand it's normal to have a gap between intention and impact. The gap is only addressable when we are aware of it.

I have also discovered some interesting patterns. For one, the strength of the relationship between the client and the stakeholder deeply matters, but maybe not in the way that you think. Most people expect more positive impact statements from the stakeholders they have good relationships with and, conversely, more negative impact statements from those with whom they have a more challenging relationship. This is a sane hypothesis, but in practice, the quality of the relationship rarely changes the substance of the *result*, though it may moderate the *intensity* of their input.

When I collect the stakeholders' impact statements, the data tends to run along a spectrum. Most stakeholders see evidence of the same blind spots, but depending on the quality of the relationship, the stakeholders may either over-index on the positive intention or over-index on the negative impact.

For example, a stakeholder who likes my client will *assume* good intentions and overemphasize the client's intentions while downplaying the impact. This leads them to tolerate some of the negative impacts caused by the blind spot.

The reverse happens too. Some stakeholders will overemphasize the client's negative impact, ignoring good intentions completely, because they have not had positive interactions with the client. This is the complexity of how the human mind discerns someone's intention versus their impact and whether they can see positive intention by giving people the benefit of the doubt.

This is where having specific examples helps as well as having three categories of stakeholders represented: (1) people with a favourable disposition to my client, (2) people who are more neutral, and (3) people with an unfavourable disposition to my client.

As mentioned above, the same blind spots generally appear across the spectrum of stakeholders interviewed, which is often surprising to my clients. All three categories will share examples pointing to a similar blind spot, just with different intensity. The great news about this is that when my clients alter their behaviour to address their blind spots, the quality of *all* their relationships improves, including the ones that were strong to begin with. They will often turn foes into friends and fans into admiring followers.

Below are some examples of questions I use in my impact-interview process. Notice how the questions begin with *positive* feedback and then lead to *opportunities for growth*. It is critical to capture a leader's strengths first because we want them to keep and enhance these. It is also very common for a development area to be linked to the *overuse* of a strength. Although some feedback may be difficult to hear, it is always more palatable when the leader understands how it is tied to their strength. There is also an opportunity to apply other strengths to drive better outcomes.

Sample Impact Questions

- What do you most appreciate and value about working with this person?

- What are examples of great contributions they make to the organization or team?

- What is an example of a situation where you have seen them at their best?

- What is an example of a situation where you think they could have done something more or differently to enhance their contribution or positive impact?

- What is an example of a situation where they may have been able to enhance their collaborations, effectiveness, and trust?

- If they were to add even more value to the organization, what might this look like?

One important note on using these questions for your own team: team blind spots are always best discovered in team discussions, while personal blind spots should be addressed during one-on-one discussions. In other words, don't take these questions into a team meeting and say, "Hey, team, today we're going to help Joe uncover his blind spots." I know that sounds like common sense, but it never hurts to mention it because it can be too easy for a team meeting to turn into an uncomfortable situation if these questions get directed at just one individual in the room.

Sample Team Questions

Here are some questions that can be used with your team to uncover team blind spots:

- What do we most appreciate and value about working on this team?

- What are examples of our greatest contributions as a team?

- What is an example of a situation where we were at our best as a team?

- What is an example of a situation where we could have done something more or differently to enhance our contribution or positive impact?

- What is an example of a situation where we may have been able to do something more or differently to enhance our collaborations, trust, and effectiveness?

- If we were to add even more value to the organization, what might this look like?

Self-Reflection

Here's the hard part. Ready? It's up to *you* as a leader to make vulnerability okay before you can ask your people to be vulnerable. This is deep work. It requires tapping into one's self-awareness *and* others-awareness, asking hard questions, and making changes based on what you uncover. As you know, change takes an open mind and a conscious commitment to evolve as a leader. It doesn't happen overnight, but when leaders make it to the other side, the return on investment is phenomenal.

Making it safe to uncover blind spots by seeing *your* own blind spots goes a long way in creating a culture where others are willing to address theirs. This truly is transformational, both on a personal level and throughout the entire company.

To start right now, consider asking yourself the following questions about the seven key blind spot areas to illuminate every corner of your brain where one might be hiding. If you'd like, you can also use them in a group setting to guide your team through some self-reflection.

False Assumptions

Your brain has formed false assumptions based on past experiences that seem similar to your current situation.

The shift you need:	Make your subconscious assumptions *conscious* to validate or challenge them.
Self-reflection questions:	• What past experiences do I think are most similar to my current role, project, or other challenge I am facing? • What expectations or approaches am I assuming to be correct but have not confirmed with others? • What assumptions might I need to validate? Who can I ask to validate or debunk them?
Team-reflection questions:	• What past experiences does our current project, mandate, or challenge most remind us of? • What expectations or approaches might we be assuming to be correct even though we have not confirmed them or considered alternative approaches? • What assumptions do we wish to validate? Who can act as our advisors or mentors to validate or debunk our assumptions or expectations?

Unhealthy Detachment

You're unaware of or ignoring your stakeholders' priorities and emotions.

The shift you need:	Realign your efforts to accommodate the key priorities of others.
Self-reflection questions:	• What does this role need me to be passionate about? • What do my colleagues and team members need me to be focused on? • What outcomes are most important to others? • Who can help me better understand which priorities have the lowest impact and highest impact?
Team-reflection questions:	• What does the organization need our team to be passionate about? • What do our key stakeholders need our team to be focused on? • What outcomes are most important to each of our stakeholder groups? • Who can help us better understand which of our priorities have the lowest impact and highest impact on them?

⊚ Differing Views of Success

You're focused on a different goal than others.

The shift you need:	Take a step back to recalibrate and align on a target that enables mutual success.
Self-reflection questions:	• What does success look like to me in my role? • Who are all the stakeholders who will judge my success? • What is their definition of success for my role? • What trade-offs do I need to balance so I don't overdo it?
Team-reflection questions:	• How do we define success as a team? • Who are all the stakeholders who will judge our success? • What is their definition of our success as a team? • What trade-offs do we need to balance between stakeholders?

Outdated Core Beliefs

You have a belief that was true at one point, but now it needs to evolve.

The shift you need:	Upgrade your beliefs by replacing them with more relevant or empowering ones.
Self-reflection questions:	<ul><li>How do my beliefs need to adapt to my current situation?</li><li>Which of my attributes do I believe are critical to my success?</li><li>Which of these may be outdated or are creating conflict?</li><li>Where do I need to give myself permission to change?</li></ul>
Team-reflection questions:	<ul><li>What beliefs do we hold as a team that we might need to adapt?</li><li>Which attributes do we hold dear and believe are critical to our success?</li><li>Which of these may be outdated or are creating conflict?</li><li>Where do we need to give ourselves permission to change or experiment with new ways?</li></ul>

 ## Unconscious Habits

You're unaware of destructive behaviours that negatively impact your effectiveness.

The shift you need:	Realize and change a destructive-habit pattern by replacing it with a new habit.
Self-reflection questions:	• What regular actions do I take that might negatively impact others? • Which of my regular behaviours are negatively impacting my mood or productivity? • What activities am I *not* doing that could positively impact my mood or productivity? • What self-care habits am I practicing or not practicing?
Team-reflection questions:	• What activities do we undertake that might negatively impact others? • What tasks or situations negatively impact our productivity? • What activities are we avoiding that could enable us positively? • What housekeeping habits are we not practicing that would benefit our collaborations?

Triggers from Past Pain

You have residual self-protection instincts that are no longer relevant.

The shift you need:	Recognize that you have a scar, but you are no longer under a threat and don't need to protect yourself.
Self-reflection questions:	• What negative outcomes am I secretly afraid of and determined not to repeat? • Where have I been taken advantage of or wronged in the past that I am trying to prevent? • Where do I lack trust in myself, in others, or in my life circumstances? • Are there any specific events, words, or images/sounds which seem to send me off the "deep end"?
Team-reflection questions:	• What negative outcomes are we secretly afraid of and determined not to repeat? • Where have we been taken advantage of or wronged in the past that we are trying to prevent from happening again? • Where might we lack trust in ourselves, in others, or in our circumstances? • What are our triggers as a team? What events, words, or situations irritate us?

Mismatched Mindsets

Your behaviours, motivations, and values aren't matched with the level of your role.

The shift you need:	Shift your mindset and values to the appropriate place for your career level.
Self-reflection questions:	• What personal ambitions am I striving for? • Do my actions show I am helping others or only helping myself? • What collaboration and culture do I want for my teams? • Given my role, where should my focus be?
Team-reflection questions:	• What team aspirations are we focused on? Are these the right ones? • Are we helping the larger organization? Where are we too focused on our agenda? • What collaboration and culture are we creating as we work with others? • Given our influence, where should our focus be to maximize a positive lasting impact?

The Takeaway

As you know, the blind spots left unchecked have the capacity to do more damage to individuals, teams, and organizations than many external forces can. When you make blind spots visible, you take away their destructive power and can move forward to become a stronger person and stronger organization.

Remember, blind spots by nature are hard to spot on your own. That's why I've made it my mission to help others find them. If you're feeling overwhelmed and unsure of how to take the right next steps, I'd like to offer you more support:

 Download a free copy of a PDF Summary of **Questions for Spotting Blind Spots** at www.leaderley.com/questionsforspottingblindspots

I absolutely love working with people who are curious about what they can do better and are open to the process of finding and fixing their blind spots.

If you're ready to jump into that process, then I want to invite you to **schedule a consultation with me**. Let's have a conversation to see if it makes sense to work together in helping you or your team identify and address blind spots.

www.calendly.com/murray-marisa/
30-minute-video-conference

Since everyone loves a good statistic, here are the top three results my clients have shared with me:

1. Ninety-two percent confirm this process improved their professional relationships.

2. Ninety-one percent say it brought clarity to their vision and improved their impact.

3. Eighty-three percent felt an increase in their confidence, awareness, and effectiveness as a leader.

As we've seen throughout our discussion, there is a *ton* of overlap between these blind spots, which is a good thing, because it means if you are able to address even just one, you can also start addressing any others.

It's worth the reminder here: *we all have blind spots.* I've got them, you've got them, and your favourite leadership expert has them. If you can create your own reflection first by hypothesizing, acknowledging, and accepting your blind spots, it empowers you to find and fix them too.

YOUR NOTES

....
....
....
....
....
....
....
....
....
....
....
....
....
....

 INTRODUCTION

BLIND SPOTS

FALSE ASSUMPTIONS

UNHEALTHY DETACHMENT

DIFFERING VIEWS OF SUCCESS

OUTDATED CORE BELIEFS

UNCONSCIOUS HABITS

TRIGGERS FROM PAST PAIN

MISMATCHED MINDSETS

UNCOVERING BLIND SPOTS

CONCLUSION

CONCLUSION

The Other Side of the Fog

Before we end our discussion, there are a couple of things I'd like to do. First, I want to sincerely thank you for reading this book. I know you're busy, and of the millions of books about leadership and corporate transformation you could have given your time to, you gave your time to me. It's one thing to start reading a book, but it's truly an accomplishment to actually finish one. So, if you made it here, I truly can't emphasize enough how much that means to me—and how much you should pat yourself on the back for making it here!

Second, I want to end with some encouragement. Facing our blind spots shouldn't be the scariest thing we do as leaders—it should be the coolest, most exciting part of our jobs. It requires the exact type of courage and kindness the world needs. The openness and curiosity required to *choose* to see your blind spots is extremely laudable.

The question now is what will it take for you to overcome them now that you see them? What is the Achilles' heel holding you back? How can you take the data points you receive from feedback and move from the reaction of "How dare you?" to "Thank you!" How can you move from being defensive and offended to connected and compassionate?

Even if you're able to answer those questions and see the obstacle in your way, this is where all of us sometimes need a helping hand to guide us over the obstacle. It's not weakness to ask for help. In reality, asking for help is often the path to tapping into new strength. It's the reason I ended up becoming an executive coach.

When I was a corporate executive, I went through three executive coaching programs over a ten-year period. All of them were helpful in various ways and helped me become a better leader, but there's one thing none of them did: they didn't help me find or fix my blind spots. They taught me best practices, how to communicate better, and how to invest in people—all worthwhile lessons—but they didn't give me the lens to see the uglier truths hiding in plain sight.

I left my last corporate executive position disgruntled and discouraged. When I mustered up the courage to quit, I felt an immediate elation of "Hurray! I'm done!" But then the next day, I found myself sitting on the floor, scared and depressed, faced with a parade of questions pulverizing my brain:

"Oh no—what do I do now?"
"How did I even get here? What went wrong?"
"What if no one ever wants to hire me again?"
"What if someone does hire me and I just make the same mistakes?"

Once I got off the floor, though, I took a long hard look in the mirror and revisited pivotal moments in my career. I looked at where the tension and friction had been. I tried to see things through a new lens.

It felt a bit like being on the other side of a breakup. When you're in the middle of it, all you can see is the other person's faults and failures. But when the smoke finally clears, you suddenly start to realize you weren't so perfect either and ask, "What did I contribute to the mess?"

That's exactly how I felt in the aftermath. It's what I like to call the "hindsight effect." Sometimes when we're in a situation, we're so focused on our own perspective that we can't see any wisdom in the opposing point of view. Or sometimes, we even manufacture an opposing point of view when there really isn't one.

I now saw the missed opportunities I had at the job, the wisdom in the other point of view I had written off in the moment. I saw my blind spots. It was ugly. But it was also liberating.

More of this came into focus when I started coaching. I found myself confronting all my blind-spot areas and saw myself in my clients' stories. Through their journeys, I got a lens into my own and saw even *more* blind spots I had ignored at the time. I wish these blind spots had been revealed to me before they caused me so much pain. Instead, I had to work through it later and take ownership of it long after the damage was done.

That's why I'm on a mission to help others.

We all want to contribute to the big fixes, but we can't do this without making the little fixes. I find it helpful to think about the Human Colossus concept, which suggests that humanity is a collective organism comprised of billions of cells, each cell represented by a single person.[6] Your city and everything in it is the visual representation of combined human intelligence over thousands of years. We continue to evolve and build on this foundation, improving with each year.

Now if you think of the human species all as one brain that we get to cumulatively contribute to, then on a micro level, we have to look at our own ecosystem. We have to see it as many other

---

[6] Slavko Desik, "The Concept of The Human Colossus," *Lifestyle Updated*, November 20, 2017, https://www.lifestyleupdated.com/2017/11/20/ concept-human-colossus/.

brains we're hanging out with, brains with intellect we can build off of to improve the collective intelligence.

We can all have a tendency to tear down ideas because they are "too old" or even "too new," without stopping to capture the brilliance in the idea and what we can gain from it. We may still disagree with others on the best way forward, but we might also discover a better way when we allow ideas to marinate together.

As I shifted gears into executive coaching, I witnessed the powerful impact of my clients recognizing their blind spots. I saw the wisdom they extracted from the feedback they received from others. I watched in awe as their blind spots became their breakthrough. They could see the opportunity hiding within the blind spot and had the bravery to experiment by shifting their approach.

Welcome the discovery. Seek out the unknown.

Like the Human Colossus, there is wisdom in the minds of those around you. Now you have the tools to capture it. These seven blind-spot areas are incredibly prevalent and common, validated by thousands of interviews across hundreds of companies. The categories are meant to serve as your guide for reflection so you can find the patterns in the blind spots, identify the problems quickly, and solve them.

As you've seen, this can be an emotional process. People can experience some big reactions when confronted with their impact statements. Confusion, anger, fear, embarrassment, betrayal—all of these are signs of fog. When you don't understand someone else's impact statement, it demonstrates that you can't see the blind spot yet. In the coaching process, I help people clear the fog to understand what's really being said in the impact statements. When we clear the fog, we find the iceberg.

One of my clients said it best: "The feedback was tough to take in. It was surprising to hear that [others] seem to experience the opposite of what I strive to do. But this process, more than any other, gave me so much to think about and was so worth it in the end."

Like navigating a ship through a fog, you've got to slow down at first. As a coach, I become a second set of eyes to aid in the navigation—to not only spot the iceberg but find the best route around it. Turning starboard won't help you if there's another iceberg blocking the path.

I hope you've also seen throughout this discussion how doable this all is. It's not an impossible task by any stretch of the imagination. Maybe you've seen yourself in one of these "characters" I've introduced. I feel like I've been every one of these character profiles at least once in my career. I've been territorial, a worrier, a know-it-all, an overachiever—you name it. If anything, this has only helped me have more empathy for my clients.

The key I've found with all my clients has been tying their blind spot to their strengths—to use their strengths as a pivot point to shift from the negative aspects of their profile back to the positive aspects. It's truly amazing how small tweaks in applying their strengths and learning a few new tools unlocks higher performance and wellness.

If you walk outside at night and carry a flashlight, it's always going to cast a shadow. It's the same in this process. Be aware of the shadows your strengths might cast, and shift accordingly. In your car, there's always a blind spot—which is why you've learned to always check over your shoulder before changing lanes. It makes you a better driver.

It does not matter where you are right now in your career—on top of your game or on the floor like I was a few years back, wondering what went wrong. I promise that with some help, you can figure this out. Even if you feel like you've already crashed the car, there is still a path to take. Sometimes we learn the hard way. You're not alone—even if it feels like it.

Start with the reflections I've included within this book—they will help you find the start line. Like any great athlete when the stakes are high, you might appreciate a coach to get you over the plateau. Even the greatest ship captain in the world needs a navigator to help them through the fog. If you're ready to see how coaching can help you navigate through the fog to find and fix blind spots, then use this QR code that links to my website www.leaderley.com to see if **working together makes sense.**

On the other side of the fog, there is an ocean of opportunity.

Today's frustration can unlock tomorrow's potential.

Your blind spot is your breakthrough.

YOUR BLIND SPOT IS YOUR BREAKTHROUGH

Thank you for investing your time with me in reading this book! I'm hoping that you are inspired to uncover the blind spots that may be holding you back from achieving your full potential.

If you would like my support and guidance throughout this process, please reach out at marisa.murray@leaderley.com

I personally collect 360 feedback, deliver executive coaching programs, and provide training, webinars, workshops, or keynote speeches on this topic. My coaching and consulting mandates bring these tools to you and your teams. Our work together has ripple effects and accelerates the success of your team and your organization.

Or perhaps you would like to inspire others to read this book to help them open up to discovering their own blind spots. One of the best ways to do that is to leave a review on amazon.com/author/MarisaMurray and share your recommendation with your colleagues and other readers.

Congratulations on completing this important first step. I wish you much success in applying your learning.

A SPECIAL THANK YOU!

Marisa dedicates 5% of all her revenues to a for-purpose (not-for-profit) organization.

Her current beneficiary is
www.aweglobal.org
An organization dedicated to taking Action for Women's Empowerment through entrepreneurial training for women in economically challenged regions in the developing world.

With the purchase of this book you too have contributed. Thank you!

ACKNOWLEDGMENTS

There are so many people who encourage and support me as I continue to grow my company, Leaderley International. I would like to thank my clients and my collaborators for their trust in our work together. My clients are the heroes in this journey. I also deeply appreciate the support and guidance I receive from a team of contributors, advisors, teachers, and fellow entrepreneurs. I would like to acknowledge these individuals for their support and contribution to this project:

Angelique Rewers and Phil Dyer — BoldHaus

Ann Gomez and Susan Pons — Clear Concept Inc.

Chidi Osirike — Social Media Curator

Eric Edmeades — Wildfit

Jonathan Jordan — Storyteller, Wordrobe Media

Maksym Sopov — Graphic Designer

Michelle Kulp — Best Selling Author Program

Sam Horn — The Intrigue Agency

Shirzad Chamine — Positive Intelligence

Vishen Lakhiani — Mindvalley

And most especially, my family, my friends, and team.

54401232R00150